DATE DUE

DEC 1 0 1979		
FEB 2 5 1980		
NOV 17 1980		
JUN 2 4 1985		
MAR 1 6 1987		
FEB 2 5 1991		
NOV 0 4 1991		
JAN 1 1 1993		
APR 1 2 1993		

DEMCO 38-297

D1286741

SHAKESPEARE IN HIS TIME

In her days every man shall eat in safety
Under his own vine, what he plants : and sing
The merry songs of peace to all his neighbours '
Henry VIII

Shakespeare
IN HIS TIME

IVOR BROWN

GREENWOOD PRESS, PUBLISHERS
WESTPORT, CONNECTICUT

Library of Congress Cataloging in Publication Data

Brown, Ivor John Carnegie, 1891–
   Shakespeare in his time.

   Reprint of the ed. published by T. Nelson, London.
   Includes index.
   1. Shakespeare, William, 1564-1616--Contemporary
England. I. Title.
PR2910.B67 1976   822.3'3   76-3664
ISBN 0-8371-8782-6

© *1960 Ivor Brown*

Originally published in 1960 by Thomas Nelson and Sons Ltd,
London

Reprinted with the permission of Ivor J. C. Brown

Reprinted in 1976 by Greenwood Press,
a division of Williamhouse-Regency Inc.

Library of Congress Catalog Card Number 76-3664

ISBN 0-8371-8782-6

Printed in the United States of America

PR
2910
.B67
1976

CONTENTS

2473383

ILLUSTRATIONS

[1] Radio Times Hulton Picture Library

ILLUSTRATIONS

Publishers's Note: The reprint edition does not include the illustrations carried on the jacket of the original edition.

PROLOGUE

To us there is a seeming contradiction about the world in which Shakespeare lived. It was in one way much smaller than our own, in another much larger. It was smaller because it was indeed Little England. During the previous centuries the English had been used to owning parts of France ; before the victories of Joan of Arc they had held quite a large part. These territories dwindled during the fifteenth century and vanished altogether with the loss of Calais in 1558 during the reign of Queen Mary. In the reign of James I outpost settlements were established with great difficulties and privations on the eastern shore of America, but they were small and in constant danger. So, during most of Shakespeare's lifetime, England was only part of an island, whose adventurous sailors raided distant seas but were in no sense Empire-builders.

The north of that island was held by the Scots, still a separate nation and potentially hostile. They had not forgotten their terrible defeat at Flodden in 1513 and the savageries wrought by the Earl of Hertford and his invading forces during the reign of Henry VIII. With them France was the friend and England the foe. The Welsh were less estranged : the Tudor monarchy sprang from the Welshman, Owen Tudor, who married the young French widow of Henry V and the Welsh were migrating into England where they hoped for favours under this régime. But the Irish were stubborn enemies and were subjected to English invasion and some merciless repression.

So England was isolated and it was Queen Elizabeth's triumph that she found her country lonely and weak and left it still lonely

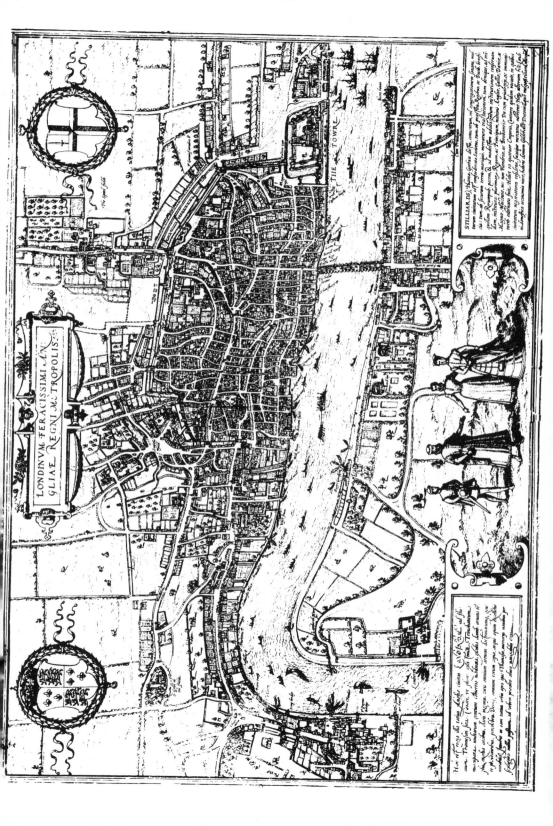

but strong. The succession of James Stuart, James VI of Scotland and James I of England, eased the relations of the two countries. Just as the ambitious Welsh had followed the Tudors to England and to London, so the Scots with an eye to advancement rode with, or after, King James on the southern road. There had also been during the century a stream of immigrants from Europe, French, Dutch, and German refugees, escaping from religious persecution. The Huguenots and others brought their various skills and crafts with them and enriched with their industry the towns where they settled. Shakespeare lodged in London with one of the Huguenot families, the Mountjoys, during the time that he was at work on some of his greatest tragedies (1602–4). Accordingly we can see that the Little England of Shakespeare's birth-time in 1564 had risen high in its status among the nations, especially after the defeat of the Spanish Armada in 1588, and had expanded in its breadth of civilisation and accomplishments by the time that his life ended.

London itself was steadily growing. An estimated population of 70,000 in the year 1500 was approaching 200,000 by 1600. But it was still, by our standards, a small town, clustered round its river. Its citizens had only to walk or ride a mile or so from the Thames to be in the country. The herb-gatherers raked the hedges of what is now Piccadilly : the sportsmen went fowling on the slopes of Islington : to the west of that lay, in Lord Macaulay's phrase, ' bleak Hampstead's swarthy moor ', a wilderness imperilled for the traveller by highwaymen, and round it was the old Forest of Middlesex, some noble remnants of which remain in the great beech-trees of Ken Wood, now part of the Heath. Shakespeare knew the word suburb, but he knew nothing of what afflicts so many of our cities and London in particular today, ' suburban sprawl '. In its place there was woodland and, where the woods had been felled, a waste. We have very few London buildings of

3

Facing page : London of Elizabeth I

Shakespeare's time : probably the scene has changed least of all in places like Epping Forest.

It was a crowded, insanitary, rat-ridden town. The rat is a plague-carrier, especially the black rat which was the chief pest and a medium for spreading the infections which came in from the ships in London's harbour : wooden houses afforded the vermin an easy home. The crowds in the close-built streets were nothing to the throngs we know today, but Shakespeare seems to have hated the pressure of a multitude. To him any popular gathering was a rank, sweaty, and stinking rabble. (He could be quite as rude about courtiers, but not for the same reason.) Our myriads are no doubt cleaner, but their swarming is far greater. In the play of *Henry VIII* there is a humorous description of the people pouring into the Palace Yard to see the great ones pass by at the christening of Princess Elizabeth. There are only a porter and his man to hold them back. ' An army cannot rule them', these lonely wardens complain, as a poor job they make of it, much to the indignation of the Lord Chamberlain.

Nowadays we would have a peacefully efficient police force to line the streets in their hundreds : and the crowds would be twenty times as large. The ' rush hour ' in a great city of today with long traffic jams, bus queues, and people milling round underground stations, would have seemed intolerable to Shakespeare. The Elizabethan standards of crowding were gentle when matched with ours. There was much turbulence when the apprentices ran riot on their holidays, but one does not hear of favourite actors being mobbed by their hysterical admirers and so jostled by ' fans ' falling on their necks that the beloved ones went in danger of bodily damage. Were Shakespeare and his fellows ever trampled on by hunters of an autograph ?

The ideas of multitude were small as the city itself was small. To us, there is amazing littleness in many parts of the Elizabethan picture. The armies were small and, to judge by old suits of armour and other costumes, the people themselves were smaller than ourselves. The seamen crossed the unknown oceans in ships that we should regard as too tiny for a fishing voyage. It may well be asked why this England has also been described as in some ways larger than our own. The answer lies in the concept of distance.

It has been the achievement of our time, or rather of quite recent time, virtually to abolish distance. That may or may not be to our real advantage, but, whether we like it or not, speed is one of the chief factors in Progress in the eyes of most people. To send a 'sputnik' hurtling round the globe in a few hours is considered a feat that all nations should emulate. Shakespeare's elvish spirit, Puck, claimed to make that circuit in forty minutes, but that was play-stuff and fairy-talk. For the highest, as well as the humblest, the pace of a horse was the extreme tempo of life. We can fly to most parts of Europe in a few hours, and we are continually delighted if some minutes are knocked off the hours. Everything and everybody must go faster and faster, whether it be the human runner knocking another second off his four-minute mile or an aeroplane crashing through the sound-barrier.

To understand the Elizabethan world we have to visualise a society in which speed was impossible and therefore not a matter for concern. We are always worrying about the saving of half a minute, though what we do with the half-minute is not always impressive. Shakespeare had not that sort of urgent thrift in mind. Distance was then a stern reality instead of being completely conquered. Thus Little England was a very big place indeed to any traveller. To go to sea was to undertake a most dangerous battle with unpredicted winds and weather and with an unknown wilderness of waves. A mile was not something that flicked by in a few seconds : it was a stubborn length of land or water. The Cotswolds in Gloucestershire seem gentle, rolling, nearby country to us :

Shakespeare, putting Bolingbroke and his forces in this region in the play of *Richard II*, sets his scene in the wilds, not the wolds, and makes a speaker say

> These high wild hills and rough, uneven ways
> Draw out our miles and make them wearisome.

The Pedlar Autolycus in *The Winter's Tale* sings, ' Jog on, jog on, the foot-path way', and adds that a merry heart will go all the way, while the sad heart tires in a mile. But that was the view of a jesting knave in a romantic comedy. The real wayfarers of the time knew a mile to be a mile.

This made England seem vast in another way. We are accustomed to the almost instantaneous dispersal of news. Not only do we get the papers, morning and evening, printed and delivered with remarkable speed : ahead of them is the information spread by radio. This applies not to our own affairs only but to happenings all over the world. Puck's forty-minute global travel has been outpaced by telegraphy and the wireless. But for the Elizabethans news, like people, moved with the capacities of the horse. Very great events, like the defeat of the Spanish Armada, could be announced by the kindling of beacons on a chain of hill-tops from coast to coast and from Kent to Cumberland where ' the red glare on Skiddaw' passed the news to Carlisle and the Scottish border. But beacons had to be prepared in advance and bad weather could seriously interfere with this service : they were only useful when something was expected to happen and the fuel prepared.

The ordinary news and reporting of the unforeseen event depended on the human messenger and the organisation of teams of ' post-horses'. However good these arrangements, the carrying of important information was inevitably slow. When Queen Elizabeth died in 1603, Sir Robert Carey had his horses posted

Silver Terrestrial Globe
The work of Paolo da Furlani of Verona, an engraver active in the second
half of the sixteenth century. The Globe, which is hollow, may have
contained a watch or other instrument

for his ride from Richmond to the Palace of Holyrood in Edinburgh, where he told James of Scotland that he was James of England too. This was a journey of four hundred miles, but with his plans for relief-horses well made, Carey managed, despite a tumble, to cover the ground between early on Thursday morning and late on Saturday night. He must have needed refreshment and a comfortable bed on arrival.

Perhaps a life of this kind, with its separations and isolations, was in one way healthier and happier than our own. It is no unmixed advantage to live at the end of a telephone and by the side of a radio or television set. With our newspapers as well we are incapable of escaping from and forgetting the pressure of events which may be ugly, evil, and menacing occurrences. Our nervous system gets no holiday. On the other hand, when there is no certain news, the power of rumour is the greater and rumour can be false and frightening. Shakespeare was alive to that peril. The prologue to the Second Part of his chronicle play of *Henry IV* is spoken by an actor masquerading as Rumour in a cloak ' painted full of tongues '. He confesses the dangers of the spoken word.

> Upon my tongues continual slanders ride,
> The which in every language I pronounce,
> Stuffing the ears of men with false reports.
> I speak of peace, while covert enmity.
> Under the smile of safety, wounds the world :
> And who but Rumour, who but only I,
> Make fearful musters and prepar'd defence,
> Whilst the big year, swoln with some other grief,
> Is thought with child by the stern tyrant war,
> And no such matter ? Rumour is a pipe
> Blown by surmises, jealousies, conjectures,
> And of so easy and so plain a stop
> That the blunt monster with uncounted heads,
> The still-discordant wavering multitude,
> Can play upon it.

8

He ends,

> And not a man of them brings other news
> Than they have learn'd of me : from Rumour's tongues
> They bring smooth comforts false, worse than true wrongs.

So, after all, the destruction of distance by our modern implements of mass-communication is, in general, a good servant of society. They may keep us ' on edge ', and some of the facts thus swiftly distributed may be proved wrong later or may be twisted by interested people for national or political purposes. But, on the whole, we are kept reasonably well informed and not left defenceless when ' loud Rumour speaks ' and his whispers go, with mounting errors and exaggerations, ' from the orient to the drooping west '.

To understand Shakespeare's age we must radically readjust our notions of population, transport, and communication. We move back into a lesser and a static England. But, if physical motion was slow, the mind was running fast and spirits high. Crowds were small, but new notions and fashions came flocking in. We must read and visit Shakespeare's plays in the light of the centuries and it is exciting to discover how much light Shakespeare himself throws on the stage of social history.

CHAPTER ONE

The Swelling Scene

IN his play of *Hamlet* Shakespeare introduced a team of actors, men of his own profession. Shakespeare's views of his craft are there revealed, since he explained his opinion of 'the purpose of playing'. Hamlet gave the players some interesting advice. They may not have welcomed it as coming from an amateur, but they had to accept it politely since it was coming from a Prince. In the course of warning them against exaggerated gestures and roaring of their lines—'ham' acting as it is called in our modern slang—he said that one of the actor's duties was to show 'the very age and body of the time his form and pressure'.

Pressure, presumably, here means a stamp or a mould. Shakespeare, by using the word 'his' instead of 'it' in front of 'form and pressure' was regarding the 'body of the time' as something colourful and personal, like a figure in a portrait. The drama, he further said, is to hold the mirror up to nature, which includes human nature, and the actors must consider themselves 'the abstracts and brief chronicles' of the time. This last remark makes it plain that he regarded the stage as both making and recording history. The drama was not just happening in a void or as a piece of entertainment unconnected with the nation's way of life.

So, when we read his plays in book-form or see them on a stage, we are not only surveying English Literature in one of its most exciting or amusing forms : we are being carried back into our own past. It is always wise to read the literature of a nation together with the political and social history of the same period. We can more easily understand what the rulers were trying to do and perhaps successfully doing, if we know what the poets of that period were imagining and the prose-writers were seeing, foreseeing, and advising.

Judging, then, by his own words about the theatre and its workers, Shakespeare regarded his own writing for the stage as, at least in part, topical. Posterity, accepting the memorable tribute paid by his occasional colleague and sometimes rival, Ben Jonson, has seized on the phrase, ' He was not of an age, but for all time.' Because Shakespeare's plays have had such enduring life, far out-ranging in esteem and popularity those of his contemporaries, and because Jonson used that phrase, people have been apt to think of Shakespeare as not representing his own century or the half-century (1564–1616) during which he lived. Yet it is made certain by his own words, just quoted, that he saw his task as that of putting the portrait of an age into the frame which his theatre provided.

It is true that most of his subjects were drawn from bygone history and old story-books. Only in one play, and that probably a specially commissioned and very quickly-written comedy, *The Merry Wives of Windsor*, did he directly portray English life and English families of the middle class from which he sprang. In his plays he is usually showing us mediaeval France or Italy, and some-times ancient Greece and Rome. In our own theatre, on the other hand, most of the plays concern our own time and our own habits.

But, while the label on the Shakespearian parcel may be that of Athens or Messina or Navarre, it will be found that most of the contents, especially the comic contents, are essentially English. Moreover, the political and social opinions of the characters, even if these people are as old and remote as the Greeks and Trojans, turn out to be closely relevant to the Courts of Queen Elizabeth I and King James I. We may surmise that if Shakespeare had known what Ben Jonson was going to write about him later on, he would have been gratefully surprised at the generous warmth of Ben's praise, but somewhat annoyed at the implication that he was not a man of his own age. Doubtless Jonson did not really mean to separate Shakespeare from the decades of his working life, from the Midland country in which he grew up, and from the city of London in which he made his income and his name. Jonson was contrasting the fame that sinks after a man's death with the larger glory that endures.

But this immortality, and the fact of there being so many alien places and themes in Shakespeare's plays, while his fellows frequently wrote comedies of London life as they knew it, have created a notion that Shakespeare was altogether too big to be a man of his own time and that we need not look to his plays to learn about the creed, character, and customs of a remarkable and renowned epoch in our history. But the passage in *Hamlet* plainly shows that he, as actor and author, was definitely engaged in providing an abstract of the aims and achievements of his own world and a brief chronicle of its qualities.

There are times when man's progress down the centuries appears slow to us as we look back into the shifting panorama of world history. The human race, or that section of it whose events we are studying, may seem, over many years, to make little or no development in thought, discovery, and achievement. Sometimes there is actually retreat instead of advance. There have been great stretches of time in which people invented and improved very little, possibly not at all. After the ancient Greek civilisation, of the fifth and fourth centuries before Christ, had collapsed in a welter of civil and foreign wars, and again after the decline and fall of ancient Rome, there were great gaps and dark ages.

The mediaeval culture arose in its beauty of building and with its great cathedrals hundreds of years after a long period of stagnation. Still books and reading were scarce ; play-acting and mummery of a kind continued at popular feasts and revels, but, except on religious subjects, there were not the specially written plays which we call ' the drama '. The invention of printing and its practice by Caxton in the fifteenth century in England did at last provide a new source of books which replaced lonely manuscripts. The flow of books later on began to grow from a trickle to a stream, and the lordly owners of the great country castles and town houses began to have libraries for their studies as well as larders for their stomachs.

When Chaucer (who lived about 1340–1400) wrote his racy *Canterbury Tales* he was picturing a society which had woken to a new life. The darkness was over : man had a light in his eyes. There was not, so far, any scramble of what is called, often perhaps too hopefully, Progress. But things were moving and they moved much faster when the sixteenth century was reached. That was the century in which William Shakespeare was born (1564) and lived the greater part of his too-brief life. He died, aged 52, in 1616. The Age of Shakespeare was one of movement in all the activities of man ; people were constantly learning more, attempting more, and enjoying more.

Of course the speed of change then was trifling if matched with the pace of alteration in our own time. We of the twentieth century have been privileged or doomed—events will settle which—to live our lives in a whirl of new powers, new inventions, new practices, and new ideas. There has never been anything like this tornado of innovation in the world before. Our generations are unique in the shifting, varying conditions of their existence. Within the lifetime of one who considers himself to be nearer middle age than old age, all conditions of social life have undergone changes as drastic as they have been swift. Many of us feel dizzy with the speed of this mad whirl of scientific and technical creation.

There was no need to feel dizzy in the reign of Queen Elizabeth I. But there was good cause for wonder and delight. The English of

Male costume in sixteenth century

Shakespeare's time were rapidly altering many of their habits and activities because the people of Europe had been making so many alterations in theirs. A hundred years before Shakespeare was born there had been a rediscovery of the ancient Greek and Roman civilisations. This has been called the Renaissance, which means the Re-birth. Thus very many things which had been started by the Greeks two thousand years earlier, fine ways of building as well as of thinking and writing, things long forgotten, were now taken up, restored and recreated with great energy and eagerness. The arts of painting and of architecture throve ; there was also a great wave of new luxury. Clothes and ornaments became much more elaborate and costly. The Italy of this Re-birth was a busy workshop of the useful and the elegant, and the eyes of England were on Italy.

It cannot be said that human conduct was equally improved ; there was a lust for power which led to envious hatreds and so to conspiracy and murder, as may be seen from the Italian stories on which Shakespeare often drew for his plots. Passions ran high and were unchecked. But at the same time there was a notable advance in learning and in craftsmanship. If a Renaissance Grandee was by no means a good example morally, he was usually a man of plentiful ideas and a devoted lover of the arts ; he may have had many bad qualities in his behaviour, but he had excellent taste in his pursuit of a colourful and richly-decorated life.

It took some time for these new skills and customs and forms of cleverness to cross the sea and captivate the English mind. But by the middle and end of the sixteenth century, that is to say the time of Shakespeare's education and of his entry to a career as poet and playwright in London, the transformation of English life had been far-reaching. There were new social ambitions and there was a great desire among those who had the means for travel to go sight-seeing in this new and glittering world of Europe reborn. There was also a keen readiness to bring home and to display the fruits of this journeying. Indeed, the travelled man, who came back with all sorts of strange notions in his head and with long new words on his tongue, was one of the jokes of the time.

Shakespeare himself may or may not have travelled in Europe, either as a touring actor or in the company of a noble patron, during the years of his early manhood about which nothing certain is known. What is quite plain is that he was ready to laugh at the pretentions and the vanities of those who had been abroad, who wanted the people at home to know all about it, and who jeered at the simplicity of all things native and at the ignorance of the English stay-at-homes concerning this ' brave new world '.

15

Rosalind, the heroine of *As You Like It*, mocks 'Monsieur Traveller' with his lisp, his strange suits of clothes, and his 'disabling' (dispraise) of his place of birth. Unless this 'Monsieur' came home in a very hoity-toity mood, Rosalind says that nobody will believe that he ever 'swam in a gondola', i.e., had been to Venice. The mark of one who had made the Grand Tour was to be contemptuous of poor old England.

Again in *Romeo and Juliet* Mercutio ridicules the mincing ways and modish talk of those who had been frisking in Europe. He curses them for being 'antic, lisping, affecting, fantasticoes, tuners of new accents'. They, with their new-found French ways, are denounced as 'strange flies, fashion-mongers, and *pardonnez-mois*'. Mercutio laughs at their cries of *bon* and their quarrelsome ways of showing off and flashing their swords in a brawl or a fencing-match. Incidentally, Shakespeare several times likened such 'show-off' types, the Frenchified braggarts, dandies, and poseurs, to insects, either plain flies or water-flies (gaudy dragonflies). He seems also to have been especially annoyed by precious methods of speech ; lisping he loathed.

But new ways of life were coming to Elizabethan England in larger spheres of life than changing fashions in clothes, character, and deportment. Some of the changes were all to the good. There were troubles and disturbances such as will occur in any lively society where new ideas are challenging the old. But at least the civil wars, which had been the plague of the previous century, were over. No longer did rival families of great wealth and power fight for the crown and ravage the countryside as they marched their armies of retainers and conscript-levies about the land, forcibly finding their provisions as they went. There was at least a strong monarchy, a central power, which kept the nobles in check and set up a rule of law. It was often a harsh law by our standards, but certainly it was preferable to the previous

anarchy and the recurrent slaughter and pillage and general insecurity caused by the Wars of the Roses.

This was the picturesque name given to the long struggle for
the throne between the houses of York and Lancaster, whose
emblems were the white and the red rose, flowers thorny indeed
for the common people. It mattered little to the poor which
band of titled gangsters, with their Norman blood and names
alien to the English peasant-stock, ultimately won the royal prize.
In either case the common man became none the richer or more
secure. What did matter to the people was the gaining of a general
settlement so that a farmer could get on with his work without
fear of marauding armies chasing each other across his land and
robbing his hen-roosts and his sheep-folds in the process. In
Shakespeare's work we find continual expressions of gratitude for
the ending of civil strife and for the Tudor dynasty's establishment
of internal peace and discipline.[1] In the last play that he wrote,
or to which he contributed much, *Henry VIII*, the christening of
Queen Elizabeth was staged and accompanied by a prophetic
speech from Archbishop Cranmer.

Shakespeare, of course, writing nearly eighty years later, could
easily be wise after the event, but it is worth noting that in his
praise of Elizabeth's reign he emphasises the security of the citizen's
life and property as one of the blessed changes which had come in
and stayed in during the queen's reign. Here are the exact words :

> In her days every man shall eat in safety
> Under his own vine, what he plants : and sing
> The merry songs of peace to all his neighbours.
> God shall be truly known.

[1] ' No more the thirsty entrance of this soil
Shall daub her lips with her own children's blood '
Henry IV. Act III, Scene I

Cranmer then goes on to prophesy peace and plenty under her successor, James VI of Scotland and I of England : this was tactful since James was on the throne when *Henry VIII* was written and doubtless saw the play and heard the words spoken. But it was not a forecast that was true for long, and twenty-six years after Shakespeare's death in 1616 the country had lost the safety and the songs of peace and was again enduring the shame and misery of civil war.

The words ' God shall be truly known ' must be noted. They refer to the religious Reformation which had swept over parts of Europe and had been introduced, chiefly for reasons of his own advantage, by Henry VIII. Many English people remained staunchly Catholic at great risk to their lives and property if they could be accused of breaking any of the laws. Shakespeare's mother came of a Catholic family, the Ardens, and it is argued by some that his father also had Catholic sympathies. All this, together with the poet's own beliefs, has been a cause of much dispute and we need not here investigate a problem to which no certain answer can be given. But it is obvious that this speech of Cranmer's in the play makes a confident claim that God was being more truly known in the austerity of the Reformed and Protestant Church than amid the rites and rituals of the Old Religion. There lay another of the great social changes which were imposed upon the fabric of English life during the sixteenth century.

The word ' imposed ' is a fair enough description of the way in which the New Religion arrived. But the Reformation, when imposed, was by no means unpopular everywhere. The Catholic Church had, in many places, developed lazy and selfish qualities : there had been corruption and misuse of its great wealth and power. The wealth mainly (and discreditably) passed now into the hands of the great families who supported Henry VIII in his quarrel with Rome, but with the breaking of the papal power in

England and the seizure of the lands and moneys of the monasteries came also a liberation. Thought was less restricted and education was extended and improved.

The new Church of England was itself attacked on two fronts. The Catholics said that the Reformation was a sin against God : the extreme Protestants, called Puritans, said that the reforms had not gone far enough. Thus the Anglican Church began its life with an attempt at compromise and it has carefully remained a middle-of-the-way establishment ever since. Since the English are little given to fanatical views and have usually shown a genius for compromise and peaceful settlement, this kind of Church has survived the pressure from both wings of religious sentiment. The most important of the immediate results of the Reformation was that the power of priests and clergy was diminished. Then, with the influx of the new learning and the new fashions which have already been described, the general temper of the people became more worldly.

Commerce and the arts both had a remarkable awakening. Readers of Shakespeare's plays must feel that they were written when life was opening out. The music to which the new world was moving was no longer that of the religious service : it was a dance of freedom in which ' the merry songs of peace ' mentioned by Cranmer went with a new kind of security and a new kind of prosperity. This flow of plenty did not please the Puritans who railed at the pursuit of pleasure, the relish of luxury, the indulgence in revels and play-acting, and the slackening of moral standards. If the Puritans had had their way, there would have been no theatres, and Shakespeare would have had to earn his living in his father's old craft of a country-town glove-maker or as a lawyer or schoolmaster, if he could not be satisfied with the life of a leather-worker. But, though they managed to suppress play-acting in certain areas where Puritanism was most powerful, notably in the

'Thou hast caused printing to be used'—*Henry VI*, Pt 2

City of London itself, they did not prevail outside their own boundaries.

Thus acting could be carried on in the precincts of royal Whitehall and in the north and south suburbs where the City Fathers had no say in the matter. Most country towns also welcomed strolling players. The Queen and many of the noblemen, as well as the lawyers, the students, and the majority of ordinary citizens, greatly enjoyed and encouraged new kinds of entertainment. They heartily disliked interference with their arts and revels and defeated the eagerness of one sect to suppress the pleasures of many others less narrow in their views. Thus it was open to Shakespeare to mock 'the kill-joys', and to say that their sour hatred of fun must not be allowed to deprive all England of its cakes and ale.

In this ferment of fresh studies and pursuits many new schools were opened : the flow of ideas, as well as of printed books, led to improved teaching. We should not now call the schools of Elizabethan England liberal or advanced : the pupils were hard driven and subject to strict discipline enforced with plentiful 'jerks' of the cane or birch, as the punishing cuts or swishes were then called. But the standard of teaching progressed and the children were taken through the European culture based on Latin and Greek with thorough methods.

School was early begun and early left and the universities, if attended, were early entered. The undergraduates of those days went to Oxford or Cambridge at thirteen or so and passed out into adult life much earlier than we do now. A boy was a man at sixteen or seventeen and a girl was a woman at fourteen (Shakespeare saw nothing peculiar in Juliet's devotion and marriage to Romeo at that age). Those whose parents could afford to let them travel, encouraged the young men to go abroad and see the great tapestry of interwoven activities and recreations in this Europe of new fashions instead of staying drowsily at home. Shakespeare, in his early plays written when his own pulse of adventure was beating strongly, repeatedly stressed the advantages of travel and of a prompt approach to the fullness of living. He mocked, as we have seen, the affectations of the Frenchified fops, but he admired the lads who sailed forth using

> Such wind as scatters young men through the world
> To seek their fortunes further than at home,
> Where small experience grows.

Those were Shakespeare's words, set down to be spoken by the hairy-chested Petruchio in *The Taming of the Shrew*, but plainly they indicate the author's own idea, since this opinion is so often repeated. In another early play, *The Two Gentlemen of Verona*, there is more praise of the wide outlook and of gallant adventuring abroad. We are told that

> Home-keeping youth hath ever homely wits

and 'homely' to Shakespeare was not so kind an adjective as it is
to us. It signified dullness rather than the honest simplicity which
homeliness suggests now. We learn, again, that

> To see the wonders of the world abroad
Is better
> Than living dully sluggardised at home.

Wise fathers, in Shakespeare's opinion,

> Put forth their sons to seek preferment out,
> Some to the wars, to try their fortunes there,
> Some to discover islands far away,
> Some to the studious Universities.

Moreover, the start was to be punctually made.

> The spirit of a youth
> That means to be of note begins betimes.

The matter is summed up in a statement that life's handicap
lay for a man

> In having known no travel in his youth.

The allusion to discovery of islands far away was topical. This
was the age of the master-mariners as well as of the masters of arts.
In 1577, when Shakespeare was thirteen, Francis Drake set out on a
voyage that was to lead him across several oceans and to make him
the first Englishman who sailed round the world. The English
sea captains were not only servants of their country but privateers
who raised money at court and in the city to launch voyages which
would bring back Spanish gold or other treasures from the Indies
and so pay handsome dividends. In one of Shakespeare's last plays,
The Tempest he drew on actual events which had occurred in
'islands far away'. During a voyage to Virginia in 1609 an English

company was wrecked on the Bermudas and spent the winter there on one of the islands before escaping to the coast of America in the following year. Prospero's island in this play should, according to the plot, be in the Mediterranean : but Shakespeare seems to have had the 'Bermoothes' in mind. His early patron, the Earl Southampton, was keenly interested in the colonising of Virginia.

For reasons of profit, quite as much as reasons of Empire, the English gentry and merchants were backing the expeditions of the seamen and the settlements which followed their landings. This was all part of that refusal to be 'sluggardised at home' which Shakespeare strongly approved. In our own time we hear regrets that so many young Britons are eager to emigrate : it is not a feeling which would have been commonly found or applauded in Elizabethan England. Home scenery offered 'small experience' and it was the large and the novel experience that was sought by those setting forth from Plymouth Hoe. They roughed it abroad and afloat, but their elegance as fops at home they richly enjoyed. Sir Walter Raleigh, of whom we shall say more later, was one of the hardiest and most untiring explorers across the Atlantic ; he was, at home, a famous dandy. But when

> All the youth of England are on fire
> And silken dalliance in the wardrobe lies

they could happily endure the hurricane in cockle-shell ships and the ardours and endurances of landings on unknown shores among savage tribes of monstrous folk concerning whom rumour spoke terrible things, telling of

> The cannibals that each other eat,
> The anthropophagi and men whose heads
> Do grow beneath their shoulders.

There had been heroes before then and nobody sang the gallantry

of the breach-storming armies in France with more eloquence and conviction than did Shakespeare. But now in ' the spacious days of Queen Elizabeth ' the sailors were in the van and were the ' front-page news ' of the town in the language of today. It was Tennyson who used the adjective ' spacious ' to describe the Elizabethan epoch. Spaciousness was hardly an obvious quality of Shakespeare's London, which was a crowded, insanitary mass of narrow streets. But the word does perfectly describe the expanding magnitude of the Englishman's ambitions. He did not yet seek to invade the sky ; but his urge to penetrate (and that profitably) the mys-

' O learned indeed were that astronomer '   *Cymbeline*

teries of the globe's surface was no less pressing than is the eagerness of a would-be space traveller to be rocketed into ' the dead vast ' far beyond the confines of our well-aired and mostly habitable globe.

Another and important change that came to England during Shakespeare's lifetime was the desire of the lively spirits to do all manner of things at once. The Elizabethan loved to be a jack-of-all crafts. He was a passionate amateur—and we must remember that the word amateur does not mean a bungler but a lover. The milords from whom the courtiers of Shakespeare's time were descended, or whose place they had arrived to take, had been devotees of power, greedy for land and for the services exacted by lords of the manor. They built castles whose ruins are still peppered over our countryside ; they jousted in tourneys of arms, they hunted, they quarrelled, they plunged into civil and foreign war. But their range of activities was limited. The Renaissance had not come to tell them that a nobleman must be more than a beef-witted squire if he was to justify a name so proud.

But new learning and delight in the arts had reached both the old families and the wealthy new arrivals who had won so much by the dissolution of the monasteries, the pillage of the Church, and the new developments in domestic and overseas trade. Accordingly the man about town was not only glad to patronise

' Swords out, and tilting one at other's breast,
In opposition bloody '   *Othello*

architects, poets, and musicians : he wrote poetry and made music himself. Nowadays most people have their music laid on by radio or by a gramophone record. Thus they get the best, whether of classical or modern, the sonata or the fashionable dance-din of the moment. Of course the professional musicians are thus kept in work, some of it very profitable. In Elizabethan England there was much less professionalism, but town and country rang with the melody and song of the amateurs and there is very little to suggest that this was badly done by incompetent handlers of a lute or owners of untunable voices.

In barbers' shops the gallants waiting for their hair to be cut or their beards trimmed did not have glossy magazines supplied for thumbing over while they waited their turn ; instead there were musical instruments provided. In house-parties all were expected to take their share competently in a glee or a madrigal. The actors and the boys whom they trained were also looked to for mastery of some musical instruments and for the pleasant use of their voices.

There came a sudden vogue for reading poetry and also for composing it ; the penning of sonnets was not left to professional writers in their penurious garrets. The owner of great estates and position, when wooing a fair lady, was ready and able to do so in acceptable verse as well as in the normal way of spoken courtship. To understand the Elizabethan ideal of a gentleman's way of life we can look to Sir Philip Sidney. After education at Shrewsbury School and Christ Church, Oxford, he spent five years (1572–7) in the kind of travel that Shakespeare so keenly praised. He devised sonnets to Penelope Devereux, daughter of the first Earl of Essex ; he wrote in prose (and in the manner of the period) a famous book called *Arcadia*, and he also framed rules for the proper conduct of literature and drama in his *Apology for Poetry*. He served with skill and heroism in a European war and was killed at the battle of

Crispin de Pass inuent. excudit.

' How oft when thou, my music, music play'st
Upon that blessed wood whose motion sounds
With thy sweet fingers. . . .'   *Sonnet* 128

Zutphen in 1586, when he was only thirty-two years old. His sister Mary, who became Countess of Pembroke, maintained a salon at the great house of Wilton near Salisbury, which is now open to the public and well worth visiting by those passing that way. She was herself a writer as well as a supporter of writers, and her husband was the patron of a company of players. It is believed, though it cannot be proved, owing to the disappearance of a document, that Shakespeare was once asked to stay at Wilton when his company was giving *As You Like It*.

The Earl of Essex (1566–1601), who married Sir Philip Sidney's widow, was also interested in the theatre ; but he was chiefly a man of action and his variety of talents were shown by his selection to be a naval commander in the conflict with Spain, assisting the direction of the triumphant raid on Cadiz. Soon after, he was appointed military commander in the much less successful effort to crush revolt in Ireland. He appears in one of the Chorus Speeches in Shakespeare's play of *Henry V* as 'the general of our gracious Empress', who is expected to bring home 'rebellion broached [spiked] on his sword'. Now our fighting men are specialists on land or water or in the air. An Elizabethan, with the audacious and confident amateurism of the time, would be an admiral one year and a general the next; and he would have an eye and ear for the graces of life as well.

The virtue of humility was rarely conspicuous in these followers of adventurous careers. Essex himself was so sure of his own power and personality that he ventured, fatally in the end, to defy the Queen. It was rash indeed to be unruly before the hot-tempered and imperious Elizabeth. For she had established herself as the unchallengeable champion of the nation and won popularity for the monarchy to a degree so far unknown; and of this she was well aware. Doubtless Henry V, with his reputation for a gaily mis-spent youth and with his record of amazing victories in the French wars, had been a people's favourite; but Henry VI was a pious and peaceful creature intended by nature for a quiet life and much to be pitied for the cruel destiny which made him the victim of turbulent nobles brawling round his shaky throne. Richard III may not have been the fiend that tradition made him nor the relentless murderer who appears in Shakespeare's play of that name, but he was not a man to make the monarchy beloved. The Tudors who followed him were more feared than revered. It remained for Elizabeth to win a wide and deep affection, even love, as well as glory for the royal person. There lay another of the great changes in the English society that occurred during Shakespeare's lifetime. No baronial lions and unicorns were now fighting for the crown: the orb and sceptre were firmly held by the hand of a Queen.

She had her faults of avarice and self-will, but she was a sovereign indeed, courageous, keen in judgement of people and brilliant in diplomacy. During her long reign (1553–1603) England rose from weakness, poverty, and bitter faction to be comparatively united and undeniably a power among the nations. The might of Spain was faced and broken ; religious strife, though not ended, was mitigated. Trade expanded and the arts flourished. The praise given to her in Cranmer's speech already quoted was justified in the eyes of her people. She herself was greatly gifted. If to be brave in deed, versatile in learning, and abounding in vitality was the mark of her period, then Elizabeth was herself the true Elizabethan.

She had been strictly and amply schooled : she knew her classical languages and could speak several modern ones. She was devoted to dancing, and even in old age was eager to tread a measure and nimble in the execution of it. She was ready for all sports : she practised archery with living targets, the deer of the forest, and she was an eager spectator of the shows that seem revolting to us but were then rapturously attended by people of all classes, the baiting of bulls and bears with dogs which, like their savage victims, were horribly mauled in the process. We must admit callousness as one of the blots upon the Elizabethan scene. Public executions and public floggings, even of women, were common and popular sights. But those same people, led by this spirited Queen, would turn from these bestialities to welcome with an equal zest music, plays, and poetry of the most delicate beauty. They had universal appetites and took all courses in the banquet of life, where Elizabeth sat radiantly at the head of the table.

One more feature of this way of rich living was the delight in words. The English may have been more eager for action than for eloquence in the previous centuries ; but now they were delighting in fine speech. Their language was a double one : the nobles, whose ancestors had come over with William the Norman Conqueror, were for a long time not wholly Anglicised ; the landed gentry who led armies to fight the French had French names and French ideas, and they used French words. They were European rather than English, and their wars were not so much forms of national defence as descents on foreign territory for their own advancement in wealth and power. Their subjects were the Anglo-Saxons, with some Celtic elements, and their language was, outside Wales, the old English with its Germanic roots. It was a more concise speech than that of the gentry who, under the European influence, were rolling long, classical words on the tongue and also putting them to paper in their sonnets.

In the mediaeval religious plays, which were made up by the people for the people, we find this old and simple speech. Here are the dying words of the wicked King Herod in one of the plays given at Chester :

> I have done so much woe
> Therefore I see now coming my foe
> To fetch me to hell
> I bequeath here in this place
> My soul to be with Sathanas (Satan)
> I die, I die, alas ! alas !
> I may no longer dwell.

Nothing could be simpler than this stream of rarely broken monosyllables. Contrast that with the eloquence bestowed by Shakespeare on Hamlet when he is questioning his father's ghost :

> Let me not burst in ignorance ; but tell
> Why thy canoniz'd bones, hearsed in death,
> Have burst their cerements ; why the sepulchre,
> Wherein we saw thee quietly inurn'd,
> Hath op'd his ponderous and marble jaws,
> To cast thee up again.

Yet Shakespeare, when he chose and when he particularly wished to move his audience to pity, could use the bare and unclassical style with most poignant effect. When Hamlet is dying he speaks to his friend Horatio,

> If thou didst ever hold me in thy heart,
> Absent thee from felicity awhile,
> And in this harsh world draw thy breath in pain,
> To tell my story.

When Hamlet's life has ebbed, Horatio says,

> Now cracks a noble heart. Good-night, sweet prince,
> And flights of angels sing thee to thy rest !

Felicity, it is true, is a long and Latin word, but the rest of the vocabulary employed to make this heart-breaking farewell has a complete simplicity.

So there was this double spring of English on which any writer could draw ; and the poets were there in abundance to use those waters of the old, quiet talk and the new, resounding rhetoric. When the great flood of words came singing and sometimes roaring across this England of the Re-birth, there were not only young men who exulted in using them ; there were readers and listeners who rejoiced to see and hear them. As early as 1586, when Shakespeare was twenty-two, a book by William Webbe called *A Discourse of English Poetry* was published, and this describes the teeming output of the new printing presses and of the great choir of poets who served the printers with their rich and musical material :

> Among the innumerable sorts of English books and infinite fardles [bundles] of printed pamphlets, wherewith this country is pestered, all shops stuffed, and every study furnished, the greatest part, I think, in any one kind are either mere [pure] poetical or which tend in some respect (as in either matter or form) to poetry.

Prose, of course, was used for argument and explanation. But the people of the period appeared to believe that, when feelings were to be expressed, poetry, with its compelling rhythms and rhymes and its heightened use of language, was essential. So the London to which Shakespeare came was already a ready welcomer of all who could put to good employment this new 'alms-basket of words', and turn to eloquence or melody the moods and emotions of the hour.

With this general survey of the Elizabethan scene we can go on to look more closely into the various aspects of the society into which Shakespeare was born as a country-town boy, and in which he rapidly matured as a brilliant worker in all the phases of a theatrical career. His journey was from Stratford in poverty and hope and back to it in prosperity and satisfaction. To us, Elizabethan and Jacobean England and London, through which that journey passed, are hard to visualise and think about without the name and the elusive figure of Shakespeare coming into the picture. But it is also true that the man himself cannot be imagined or understood without the town and country that were his nurse, his workshop, and his raw material. Britain, and indeed the world, is in debt to Shakespeare for the legacy of his poems and plays : but he was indebted too. A nation which in his time was so much in love with living, so rich in characters for a playwright's portraiture, and so ready in acceptance of poets and poetry could fairly be said to have contributed its share to the glorious result.

CHAPTER TWO

Country Matters

WILLIAM SHAKESPEARE knew the lore and enjoyed the humours of the English countryside, but we must not think of him as coming from a village home ; he was a country-town boy, which is quite a different thing from a country boy. But the farms and fields were very close to his birthplace, Stratford-upon-Avon. This was a centre of marketing, of schooling, of local government, of rural business, and of legal actions. These seem to have been a plentiful source of income to the lawyers and of entertainment to those who sued their neighbours or defended themselves against suits and prosecutions. The tradesmen and farmers did not practise duelling with rapiers, like the gallants in London. But they did much fighting with writs.

The earliest-known print of Shakespeare's birthplace

Shakespeare's birthplace today

This Stratford was, by the standards of the time, a considerable place, and its way of conducting its affairs is worth inspection, not only because it was the background of one man's life that was to become world-famous, but because it was typical of the Elizabethan England which was feeding London with its ambitious and talented youth. (Many of the notable men and especially the writers of the time were not born Londoners; they came to London to discover careers and, because of their abilities, they greatly increased that city's reputation.)

Stratford's history went far back; it had been recognised as a borough since 1195; the business of the town, before Shakespeare's period, had been mainly administered by a religious body, the Guild of the Holy Cross, which cared for the poor, governed the school, and provided for the services at the Church of the Holy Trinity with priests housed in a College. The Chapel of the Guild and the

Trinity Church are still there and chief among the much-visited sights of the town. The church has inevitably undergone alterations since buildings, like men, have their maladies of old age and need doctoring. Shakespeare would not have recognised the present church tower which, replacing the ancient steeple, has long been a handsome and conspicuous landmark of the Avon valley.

The Reformation soon had its impact on Stratford, as on similar towns. The authority of the Catholic Church was ended and its properties annexed. Rule by laymen followed the rule of the clergy. In 1553 the Guild and College were dissolved and the town received a charter which gave it a measure of self-government. A Town Council took charge. This was all in accordance with the picture of English life at the time. The middle class, composed of members of the crafts and tradesmen as well as of lawyers and any other professional men, was acquiring moderate powers in proportion to its moderate importance and moderate wealth. In

The Garden of New Place, Stratford, showing the Chapel of the Guild

future the Reformed Church would have responsibility for the souls of the people, or at least for those who were not Catholic or Puritan ' recusants '. The town, its business and its amenities (or lack of them), were the care of the Council.

The population of Stratford was then about two thousand. The inhabitants of the city of London and its suburbs are supposed to have numbered about two hundred thousand. (There were no official figures compiled by accurate census.) This means that London was a hundred times more populous than Stratford, whereas today the huge mass of Greater London, home of eight million people, has a population five hundred times greater than that of the present Stratford with its sixteen thousand. Thus it can be seen that the old Stratford was arithmetically quite important. There were few big towns outside London in 1560. The chief of these were Plymouth, York, Norwich, and Bristol, whose citizens ran to about twenty thousand in each case. The great industrial cities of today were still tiny townships, and Stratford's huge neighbour, Birmingham, was yet an infant.

Those who seek to maintain that Shakespeare, being a Stratfordian, came from a village of illiterate peasants and therefore could not have become a literary man and written the plays and poems generally attributed to him, are far from accurate. There was a good school in the town and a collection of books was no rarity. The parson who christened the infant Shakespeare on 26 April 1564, John Bretchgirdle, had a considerable library and left a legacy of books to a local draper and his son, which he would hardly have done if they could not read them.

There are no signs of general illiteracy in Shakespeare's plays : obviously he did not regard servants as incapable of reading and writing. The servant characters can do both, and nobody thinks that a remarkable feat. A shepherdess in *The Winter's Tale* is eager to be given the texts of ballads for reading. The pedlar

An Elizabethan Song-Sheet
' My traffic is sheets '—*The Winter's Tale*

Autolycus does a trade in song-sheets among the country folk.
It is true that the scene of this play, which describes country life,
with its shepherd's work and revels, is set in Bohemia, but it is,
we soon discover, a very English landscape, bright with the flowers
that Shakespeare knew in Stratford ; the supposedly mid-European
rustics are essentially English yokels, and it is one of these from
whom the girl, Mopsa, begs the pedlar's sheets. ' I love a ballad
in print a-life,' she says, ' since then we know they are true.' To

37

believe everything appearing in print is a sign of simplicity, a simplicity continuing in a number of people to this day ; but it is also proof of an ability to read.

The Quiney family, next-door neighbours of the Shakespeares in Stratford, exchanged letters and we know that there was a correspondence between father and son while one of them was in London. Young Richard Quiney could write good, fluent Latin at the age of eleven. This, we may surmise, is more than could be accomplished at any age by some of those who now sneer at Shakespeare's Stratford as a home of oafs and barbarians.

There is no certain proof that William Shakespeare was sent as a boy to the Stratford Grammar School. But where else would he have gone ? His father, as a member of the Council, had a right to a free place for his son and there was no adjacent rival to that already ancient and now well-esteemed academy. Under the new régime, established in 1553, it had been reconstituted as the King's New School and was a place of importance. The headmaster was paid a salary twice as large as that usual in similar posts elsewhere. Those chosen for the position held Oxford degrees and were men of some scholarship.

The discipline in a Grammar School was severe and the hours long. Schooling began early in life, at the age of five, and the day's work began early too. The boys paraded at seven in winter and six in summer. The lessons went on, with breaks for meals, until five and these breaks were no rest for the children who were expected to wait upon their parents at table. There were two half-holidays in the week and forty days of vacation in the year. The very young went to an elementary school to learn their letters before proceeding to a Grammar School at the age of seven.

The first instruction was given with an Absey book (A B C Book) also known as a horn-book. The letters of the alphabet were printed on a single piece of paper and this sheet was then

Horn-book

set on a wooden frame with a handle below it, so that it resembled a toy bat in shape. The paper was covered with a sheet of horn which kept it clean and comparatively hard to damage or destroy.

At the Grammar School there was instruction in the Bible and Latin as well as in English. Latin was the means of international communication in Europe, and the Roman Catholic Church made knowledge of it advantageous. Shakespeare's plays show full acquaintance with the Scriptures and some of the classical Roman authors, especially Ovid. A textbook in general use was Lily's *Short Introduction to Grammar*, published first in 1567. It is quoted several times in Shakespeare's plays.

There was no idea then of making lessons easy and attractive ; nor was it thought that children had any right to be happy. School was to be school with no nonsense about it. Bad behaviour was not excused with talk of 'maladjusted types' and 'an unsatisfactory domestic background'. We can comprehend the severity of the approach to education from a book called *The Grammar Schoole*, published forty years after Shakespeare's entry to the curriculum, but probably giving a good idea of what the boys underwent in Elizabethan England.

Its author was John Brinsley, a schoolmaster in Leicestershire. His basic belief, which may be taken as commonly held, was that children were naturally vessels of original sin or at least of original naughtiness, if sin be regarded as too grave a word to be applied to a boy of seven. Children were held to be the natural prey of Satan, and the way to deal with that was to whip the devil

39

out of them. Brinsley believed that the cane and the birch were sanctified by God for the salvation of young souls through the castigation of the young body. The rod, which he blatantly called 'God's instrument', was to be applied to all 'stubborn or unbroken' boys, and the method of 'breaking' these limbs of Satan was to flay them : if one resisted this form of spiritual cure 'three or four scholars known to be honest and strong' were to 'hold him fast over some form' while the master carried out God's work. The master was only advised not to strike his victims over the head or to use violent language.

'Do it under God,' said Brinsley, 'and you shall never hurt them. You have the Lord for your warrant.' Brinsley's God of Wrath, who seems to have been no relation to Jesus Christ, was

' The threatening twigs of birch '—*Measure for Measure*

not a figure any more likely to be loved than was that odious pedagogue himself. Those who read Charles Lamb's essay on Christ's Hospital will see that Brinsley's methods lived for two hundred years after his manual for teachers was written, and there may be some dark corners where Brinsleyism still survives. But, on the whole, scholastic ideas of God's will and of the proper way to perform it have changed radically and for the better.

Henry Peacham, a schoolmaster of many accomplishments, wrote in 1634 of one of his profession who did not bother to justify his exercise of beating with talk of divine love. ' I knew one,' he tells us, ' who would ordinarily on a cold morning whip his boys over for no other purpose than to get himself a sweat : another beats them for swearing and all the while swears himself with horrible oaths.'

Shakespeare's masters and those other ushers who turned out the excellent scholars and gifted, vivacious writers of the age could defend their regimen by pointing to the results. But the pupils might have answered, with some justice, that they had managed to do well despite these methods and not because of them. Shakespeare himself showed no respect or affection for schoolmasters in his plays, and there are no fond allusions to the dear old school. We do not meet a ' Mr Chips ' in his memories of the classroom ; he laughs, instead, at ludicrous pedants, like Holofernes, in *Love's Labour's Lost*, whose conversation is full of Lily's school-book Latin and vain displays of erudition.

Nor does Shakespeare show any sympathy for the teacher who has to give instructions to a large class of dull or difficult pupils, keep his temper through a long, hot day, and maintain his faith in the virtues and merits of education at the same time. There was an old tradition that Shakespeare was himself for a while a schoolmaster in the country ; if he was, we may reasonably guess that a man of such wide sympathies could never have been one of the Brinsley type. More probably, he would have been despised by his colleagues for sparing the rod with whose discipline they were harshly active and for omitting to drive out Satan with savage methods. If Shakespeare was ever a teacher, he would surely have seen the other side of the classroom picture and understood the weariness which may accompany the giving of instruction to those who do not much care for receiving it and may actively oppose it.

At any rate his view of schooldays was plainly one of hard and rather unhappy times. Childhood he could idealise ; indeed he actually answered Brinsley's notion of original sin with his picture of guileless children untroubled by thoughts of a gloomy tomorrow and fancying themselves to be ' boys eternal '. Here is their bliss, as described in *The Winter's Tale* :

> We were as twinn'd lambs that did frisk i' the sun,
> And bleat the one at the other : what we chang'd
> Was innocence for innocence ; we knew not
> The doctrine of ill-doing, no, nor dream'd
> That any did.

Few passages are better known than the speech of Jacques on the seven ages of man in *As You Like It*. This includes the familiar picture of the reluctant scholar ;

> The whining school-boy with his satchel,
> And shining morning face, creeping like snail
> Unwillingly to school.

We can gather from this that Shakespeare's mother insisted on his leaving home at the peep of day with his face well scrubbed, even behind the ears, and with his ' prep ' done and stowed in the satchel. (The mention of that article is an indication of books taken to and from the house for ' prep ' purposes.) The snail's progress further suggests that the boy's spirits were not as brightly shining as his face and that he had no inclination to greet the morning and his masters with a cheer.

Although England had a queen who proved her range of capacities at the highest level, and in time made herself feared abroad and beloved at home, the society of which she was the head was predominately masculine. We hear very little of the education of girls, much of the schooling of boys. In the rich houses there was, presumably, private tuition and in the poor homes domestic instruction. We know that the young ladies who went to Court had their wits sharply set for an exchange of ' conceits ', that is to say of clever talk, banter, and smart retort. The heroines in Shakespeare's comedies, such as Beatrice in *Much Ado About Nothing* and Rosalind in *As You Like It*, could hold their own with any smart-spoken man in these exchanges and could draw on considerable knowledge of classical myths and legends. The shrewd Portia of *The Merchant of Venice* was far from being an unlettered lady. If the audiences had not been used to women of wide reading and of ready tongue, such characters would have seemed impossible. The plays were watched by women as well as men, and the audiences would be judges of what culture and gifts an Elizabethan lady possessed. Lower down the social ladder there were the Mopsas who, as we saw, had been taught to read.

The sons of the wealthy families usually had private tutors until they were thirteen or fourteen, and then they went straight to one of the two existing Universities, Oxford and Cambridge. (Sir Philip Sidney's schooling at Shrewsbury was an exception.) The Earl of Southampton entered St John's College, Cambridge, at fourteen, stayed there four years, and then went to study law at Gray's Inn in London.

Francis Bacon went to Trinity College, Cambridge, at thirteen and to Gray's Inn at fifteen. The Inns of Court were then really a third English university and more like the universities of our own time, since they took in their students or 'termers' at an age closer to that of our undergraduates of today. The Inns of Court men were much given to appearing in masques and to acting plays

Boy flying a kite

themselves and to attending plays given by the professional actors. Their proceedings were gay to the point of tumult. We know that on the Holy Innocents' Day in December 1594 Gray's Inn had 'Dancing and Revelling with Gentlewomen : and after Sports, a *Comedy of Errors* was played by the Players'. The play and the company were Shakespeare's. This caused great hilarity and 'The Night was begun and ended in nothing but Confusion and Errors'.

But we are wandering away from the country town, its schooling, and its recreations. Boys were forbidden 'clownish sports',

Blowing up a football

and there was to be no gambling. But athletics of all kinds were encouraged ; the organisation of these would be arranged by the participants. One does not hear of the games-master in Elizabethan academies, and the pedagogues appearing in the plays are dull-as-dust fellows and not at all the kind of men who would take an interest in the running, leaping, and swimming of their pupils. Shakespeare makes two mentions of football, once of the ball itself in a metaphor, as something spurned, and again when one man trips up another and calls him 'base footballer'. Apparently football and 'fouls' were associated in Shakespeare's mind. There is no mention of cricket except as a chirping insect, but there might have been reference to the game, for the English were already playing a form of it. As early as 1180 a rhymer called Joseph of Exeter wrote :

> The youths at cricks did play
> Throughout the merry day.

There were then two stumps with a third over the top of them and the wicket-keeper's position was not sought after ; a menial serf was brought in to be the stumper. In 1447 an edict was passed against playing cricket, just as the Scottish Kings tried to keep down their native game of golf. The reason in both cases was the same : it interfered with the serious practice of archery, a practice which was necessary for national defence.

The curate Nathaniel in *Love's Labour's Lost*, that charming ninny, is described as ' a foolish, mild man, an honest man, look you, and soon dash'd. He is a marvellous good neighbour, faith, and a very good bowler '. But this does not mean that he could spin a crafty leg-break, and he plainly was not of the physique to hurl down ' scorchers '. The reference is to bowls, a game to which

' He is a marvellous good neighbour, faith, and a very good bowler '
Love's Labour's Lost

' Give me mine angle, we'll to the river '—*Antony and Cleopatra*

there are many allusions. We know from the anecdote about Drake and his disdain of the need to set sail quickly, that, when the game of bowls was afoot, nothing else mattered. It was one of the chief Elizabethan recreations, and Shakespeare often drew his verbal images from the bias of the weighted ' wood '.

Swimming was a common exercise. The initiates made their first attempts with the aid of what we call water-wings ; boys that swam on bladders are mentioned in the play of *Henry VIII*, and Shakespeare knew that

> An unpractised swimmer plunging still
> With too much labour drowns his want of skill.

Fishing, too, was a general pastime : trout were tickled, as we say—that is, caught by the groping hand. There is talk of the care

' Thou hast hawks will soar '—*The Taming of the Shrew*

needed in baiting a hook, and the carp was regarded as a prize of a wary kind for whom a cunningly chosen lure would be necessary.

The chief field-sports of the time were ' birding ' and hunting. Birds were snared by putting lime on the branches or netted ; guns were already good enough to enable shooting. There is a vivid description in *A Midsummer Night's Dream* of

> Wild geese that the creeping fowler eye
> Or russet-pated choughs, many in sort,
> Rising and cawing at the gun's report.

But hunting and hawking were the pursuits most frequently and happily practised by the Elizabethans. Shakespeare knew all about both. Especially in the early plays, when Stratford and its countryside were warm in his mind, he repeatedly described the excitements of the chase and, with deep feeling, the pains of the chased. The Lord in *The Taming of the Shrew* argues with his huntsmen about the abilities of their hounds in picking up a scent.

> Saw'st thou not, boy, how Silver made it good
> At the hedge-corner in the coldest fault ?
> I would not lose the dog for twenty pound.

To this the huntsman replies

> Why, Bellman is as good as he, my lord ;
> He cried upon it at the merest loss,
> And twice to-day picked out the dullest scent :
> Trust me, I take him for the better dog.

Deer were plentiful in the richly-wooded England of the time and they were shot with bow and arrow or hunted with hounds. Whether or not the old tradition be true that the young Shakespeare was in trouble for poaching in a deer-park—the story is usually discredited now—it is plain that he had some knowledge of this kind of illicit enterprise. In the early play of *Titus Andronicus* it is asked

> What, hast thou not full often struck a doe
> And borne her clearly by the keeper's nose ?

The coursing of hares with greyhounds, or the hunting of them with hounds, was another favourite sport and in this case, as so often also in the case of

> The poor frighted deer, that stands at gaze,
> Wildly determining which way to fly

Shakespeare's sympathy was with the prey and not with the pursuer. There is a long and famous passage about a hare hunt in the narrative poem of *Venus and Adonis*. The purblind hare, poor wretch, tries to escape by taking a winding course and leaping sideways.

He cranks and crosses with a thousand doubles.

The hare hears the clamour of the chase and tries to throw off the scent by mixing with a herd of deer.

> By this, poor Wat, far off upon a hill,
> Stands on his hinder legs with listening ear,
> To hearken if his foes pursue him still :
> Anon their loud alarums he doth hear ;
>   And now his grief may be compared well
>   To one sore sick that hears the passing-bell.

> Then shalt thou see the dew-bedabbled wretch
> Turn, and return, indenting with the way ;
> Each envious brier his weary legs doth scratch,
> Each shadow makes him stop, each murmur stay :
>   For misery is trodden on by many,
>   And being low never reliev'd by any.

Dr Caroline Spurgeon, authoress of *Shakespeare's Imagery*, made an exact study of Shakespeare's mind and tastes as revealed in his use of words and metaphors. She concluded that the commentators who talk of Shakespeare's love of the chase have been led astray. He had seen it in all its forms, as he had watched the descent of the falcon on its prey. But, if we examine his descriptions, we get the picture of an extremely sensitive man whose sympathy is scarcely ever with the hunters but consistently and obviously on the side of the hunted or stricken animal, ' the moody-mad and desperate stag hunted even to falling'. ' So much is this the case,' concluded Dr Spurgeon, ' that out of thirty-nine hunting images I only once find the hunt pictured as a gay and joyous pastime and described from the point of view of the sportsman.'

But Shakespeare must not be regarded as typical of his time ; his perceptions were too delicate and his nature too compassionate for him to be a normal, hearty, rough-living countryman. Lords and commoners alike had no scruples about inflicting pain, and for them ' the jolly troop of huntsmen ' were congenial company. ' Poor Wat ' and the stricken deer were, in their opinion, put on earth for man's entertainment in the chase as well as for the service of his larders. Everywhere, too, the ' birding ' went on. The cult of the falcon filled man's talk with its special terms. One of Ben Jonson's characters says in the comedy called *Every Man in his Humour*, ' An a man have not skill in the hawking and hunting languages nowadays I'll not give a rush for him. They are more studied than the Greek or Latin '. Shakespeare perhaps found hawking a more tolerable pastime since the kill is quickly over. The predatory falcon appeared on his family crest when he obtained a coat of arms and the title of Gentleman for his father in 1596.

The use of the phrase ' not give a rush ', equivalent to the modern not give a bean or a damn, brings us indoors. The rushes, growing by the river or in the swampy land, were cut and dried for use as carpeting and also for working into mats and mattresses. The Elizabethans, even the wealthy ones, trod hard, sat hard, and slept hard. Rushes, unless heaped so thickly as to impede movement, would not make an adequate substitute for our pile carpets. There was a luxurious floor-covering called a Turkey mat, not necessarily imported from Turkey but wrought in rich Turkish style ; this, however, was known only in great houses. Elsewhere the rushes were strewn on the floorboards.

Even in such an aristocratic household as that of the Capulets in the Verona of *Romeo and Juliet*, Shakespeare visualised a spread of rushes in a ballroom, a covering which was not, one would think, very suitable for a dance floor. But Romeo, when declining to be a dancer and preferring ' to be a candle-holder and look on ', says

A torch for me : let wantons light of heart
Tickle the senseless rushes with their heels.

Some Tudor portraits of great personages show their subjects standing on plaited rush-mats and not amid loose rushes. There were also mats set round the altar rails in churches for kneeling worshippers. In the home, especially a country home, with people coming in and out from muddy fields and streets, the rushes had to be frequently swept up and cleaned by those who cared for cleanliness, perhaps a job for the children and not always popular.

There are examples of the rush mattress to be seen at and around Stratford in the homes of Shakespeare's family, now owned and tended by the Birthplace Trust. Beds were made by lacing strong cords between the side-rails of the bedstead and by setting the rush-mattress on the top of these. Oliver Baker, in his book on *Shakespeare's Warwickshire*, a work based on long and careful antiquarian research in the locality, states that this kind of bed and mattress were not only the simple furniture of an ordinary family. 'They were the usual foundation on which beds were placed and were often catalogued in the inventories of the great houses.' On their tombs, too, important people were often shown as lying on their mattresses, with one end folded as a support for the head. But one reads also of flock or feather mattresses, to be laid on top of the rush one by those who could afford them. On the whole, however, the Elizabethans were used to lying hard.

The principal beds were called 'standing-beds'. These were four-posters with surrounding curtains and a 'tester' or roof. The latter might be made of gaily painted cloth and be slung on finely carved posts. A bedroom of the nobility would be handsomely and expensively decorated. We get an idea of that from the bedroom in which Imogen, the heroine of Shakespeare's *Cymbeline*, slept. The time and country of this play was that of

'Although the sheet were big enough for the Bed of Ware
in England'   *Twelfth Night*

Ancient Britain, but Shakespeare was thinking of the nobility in
his own England when he described the elegance. There is allusion
to rushes on the floor, but the room

>   Was hang'd
> With tapestry of silk and silver ; the story
> Proud Cleopatra, when she met her Roman
> And Cydnus swell'd above the banks, or for
> The press of boats or pride ; a piece of work
> So bravely done, so rich, that it did strive
> In workmanship and value ; which I wonder'd
> Could be so rarely and exactly wrought ? . . .

These somewhat tangled lines suggest the intense realism of the picture. Furthermore the chimney-piece had a painted cloth or tapestry of

> Chaste Dian bathing ; never saw I figures
> So lively to report themselves.

But such trappings were only for the very eminent.

Beneath the ' standing-bed ' could be stowed in daytime the truckle-bed, a lowly article on wheels or runners which could be brought out and used elsewhere by children or servants. There was also the ' field-bed ', the Elizabethan version of our camp-bed ; its parts were separate and so it could be taken on journeys or to camp in time of war. Mercutio in *Romeo and Juliet* contrasts the discomfort of the ' field-bed ' with that of the ' truckle-bed ' to which he is going. Was this man-about-town really in the ' truckle-bed ' class ? He may have been joking. We can imagine the boy Shakespeare sleeping on a ' truckle-bed ' kept in daytime under the four-poster used by his parents, which would have few, if any, of the rich hangings and adornments described in Imogen's sumptuous room.

On the walls there was, in the homes of the prosperous, oak-panelling. The less wealthy had their painted cloths. Elizabethan England had no ample supply of framed portrait painting ; the picturing of landscape and especially of scenes drawn from the Bible and old classical legends, which were widely popular, was done on cloth. Tapestry involved so much work that it was regarded as something of a luxury : it was the painted cloth that usually did the work of wallpapers where there was no panelling to cover the naked wall.

There are many allusions in Shakespeare's plays to this form of domestic decoration in the country houses. The induction to *The Taming of the Shrew* has particular interest for students of Elizabethan England since there Shakespeare's scene is ' before an alehouse ' and

inside a lordly mansion of his own period. Inside the mansion
there are pictured hangings in rich variety available for the delight
of Sly, the drunken tinker who has been put to bed in noble sur-
roundings for a joke. The room was almost as rich as Imogen's.
He could see

> Adonis painted by a running brook,
> And Cytherea all in sedges hid,
> Which seem to move and wanton with her breath,
> Even as the waving sedges play with wind.

Or he could feast his eyes on the spectacle of

> . . . Daphne roaming through a thorny wood,
> Scratching her legs, as one shall swear she bleeds.

One has the feeling that Shakespeare is here describing cloths that
he had himself seen and appreciated. The likeness to 'the real
thing', emphasised in Imogen's case, was of great importance to
Shakespeare in his judgement of a picture; he believed that the
painter should hold his mirror closely up to nature and he would
have been shocked by our modern art which cultivates distortion
or prefers an abstract picture to exact portraiture.

The prosperous country house of the period like that of the
Clopton family or of the Lucys, near Shakespeare's Stratford, had
abundance of colour. The oak-panelling would in many cases be
quite new and therefore light in tint; the tapestries would be
freshly woven from our point of view and the pictorial cloths
on the walls would be freshly painted. In museums and ancient
houses, now on show, we are accustomed to seeing fine old exhibits
from which the original gloss and brightness have departed. We
must not think of Elizabethan England as full of rooms darkened
by ancient panelling and lacking bright hues in its textiles. The
furnishings and decorations, which we see in their old age or even

Silver Apostle
spoon

in decay, were then in the flush of youth. It was an England in full hue.

The equipment of an Elizabethan home was, like the equipment of homes in any place and period, an indication of domestic prosperity or the lack of it. This was noticeable in the plate and table furniture. The social rank, from Queen to peasant, was shown by the plates from which people ate and the ewers in which they washed their fingers during meals. Such washing was most necessary since forks were scantily used and it was customary to cut up the meat and then eat it with the fingers and to gnaw the bones. During Shakespeare's lifetime the use of forks was limited to the very elegant and refined folk, although the implement had been known in the country for some time. Ben Jonson in his *Volpone* describes a socially ambitious English traveller who, in Venice, tells another that

> You must learn the use
> And handling of your silver fork at meals.

Dishes, flagons, and basins were graded according to the wealth of the family, ranging from royal gold, to silver, pewter, and wood. The wooden ' trencher ', or flat dish, was the common implement of refreshment.

In the same way the chairs and tables were of a wide variety in workmanship ; but all showed taste. Feeble design and vulgar embellishment were to come later. One sign of wealth in a country house was the supply of handsome chairs. The poor were used to stools. The carpenters made the articles of turned wood and the joiners made those pieced together with mortice and tenon ; the old craft guilds had their own trade-union spirit and kept their own spheres of labour jealously to themselves, but the results were handsome. Chests, tables, and cupboards mingled strength and grace in their design and were often delicately ornamented with carving. That cushions were used is shown by the frequent mention of these aids to comfort in Shakespeare's plays, but he was writing mainly of the well-to-do.

There is a settee on view in Ann Hathaway's Cottage at Shottery near Stratford, and the sightseer may be led to fancy that Shakespeare did his wooing of Ann

Farthingale Chair

Hathaway thereon. But it is a grim-looking place of session and offers little room for cushions or courtship. J. C. Trewin in *The Story of Stratford-upon-Avon* wrote of this home of the Hathaways : 'I have murmured appropriately at the sight of the baking-oven with its wooden door, the four-poster Tudor bedstead of carved oak, the mattress of plaited rushes, the wooden trencher, and the rushlight holder. I have even tried to set William and Anne, in the mind's eye, on that excessively uncomfortable, straight-backed narrow settee by the parlour hearth. But this belongs to the Shakespeare Romance which has been grafted on what we know of the poet's early life.'

I agree that a modern sofa would better accommodate such romance than could this settee on which a couple of the stricter

Puritans might suitably have applied themselves to pious meditation. Sofas, known as day-beds, are mentioned twice under the latter title in the plays. But they are not in ordinary homes. The pompous steward, Malvolio, in the great house of the wealthy Olivia in *Twelfth Night* talks of lolling on his day-bed.

The bright colours of an Elizabethan home have been mentioned, but naturally only those who could afford torches, lamps, and candles in plenty had much illumination at night. For the mansion there were torches in brackets and white tallow candles with cotton wicks. These could be set in holders suspended from the ceiling and would make a pleasant, mellow light. But the normal family could not afford them : four shillings bought twelve pounds of such candles, but four shillings would be the equivalent of some seventy or eighty shillings now. The commoners had the rushlight, a home-made article in which a rush-wick was inserted in the various fats saved in the kitchen. Shakespeare thought poorly of this product. Iachimo in *Cymbeline* uses the words

> Base and unlustrous as the smoky light
> That's fed on stinking tallow.

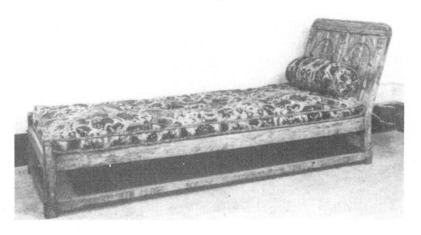

' Having come from a day-bed, where I have left Olivia sleeping '
Twelfth Night

Moreton Hall, Cheshire, showing the architecture of the
middle sixteenth century

He has several references to the flickering of a lamp ' whose wasting
oil is spent '. It was the obvious image to apply, in poetical drama,
to a dwindling life, but its recurrence suggests that the failure of a
lamp had often irritated him, perhaps when he had a book in hand
on some wintry night of his youth and was eager to read on. He
may for the same reason have been unable to continue his own
writing when he was established as an author. The brain was
racing, but the light had failed. One of the pleasures that must
have appealed to him most keenly when he entered a rich house
in the country or a mansion in town would be the escape from

'stinking tallow' to the hall well lit with its candelabra and with the torches in their sconces.

The Elizabethan world, in town as well as village, was much darker than ours. A stroll in the streets at night must have somewhat resembled a hazardous walk during the 'black-out' which we experienced during the last Great War. While the rooms in the houses were lit up there would be some beams of illumination, but they were only feeble flickerings from inadequate domestic lights : the windows were not made of the glass we know and were poor transmitters. When the inhabitants had gone to bed the belated wayfarer would have to carry his own torch or grope in the blackness.

If we think poorly of the printing work in the texts of plays of the period and are surprised at the number of errors, we must remember that the printers on a murky day or in the late afternoon of winter had no blaze of electric light with which to check a hurriedly written piece of manuscript and to carry on their own hand-setting of the type. They had only the rushlight candle with which to peer at their papers and, if they wore spectacles, these would not be as accurate or as helpful as ours. Oil for lamps cannot have been common or cheap. Whale oil was known, as we can tell from an allusion in *The Merry Wives of Windsor*. Mistress Ford says of Falstaff, 'What tempest threw this whale, with so many tuns of oil in his belly, ashore at Windsor ?' But we do not know how much of this oil there was, nor how it was distributed.

To the men of the Middle Ages cleanliness had come well behind godliness, and godliness, as we have seen, had in Shakespeare's time somewhat dwindled, except among the stubborn Catholic and Puritan circles. With the overthrow of the Old Religion a large part of the nation was developing more appetite, and finding more opportunity, for earthly pleasures.

Shakespeare himself was disgusted by dirt, and some chance remarks in the plays strongly suggest that he was especially revolted by unwashed dishes and by greasy scraps of food : the sight of ' a beastly feeder ' was abhorrent to him, which is likely enough in the case of a sensitive man. The absence of forks would naturally provoke a certain amount of beastly feeding in all ranks of Tudor society.

The bath in a country or small-town home would be water from the well, warmed up, and set in a tub by the fire in winter. A series of baths would involve a lot of work and, in the case of a large family, the tubs may have occurred at rarer intervals than we, in this well-watered and hot-watered age, would regard as sufficient.

The toothbrush was then little known, but the toothpick was in regular use, at least among the elegant. A man who lived at that time to the age of eighty-three, the Rev. Dr Blois, attributed some of his good health, which he looked after vigilantly, to his dental cleanliness. He was described as being, after meat, ' careful almost to curiosity, in picking and rubbing his teeth '. Instead of the brush normal today a cloth was used for a tooth-rub after meals. The herbalist Gerard advised scrubbing the teeth and gums with the juice squeezed out of tobacco as a good remedy for tooth-ache.

There are three mentions of toothpicks in Shakespeare's plays and a number of allusions to the toothache ; but none to the toothbrush. Some dentists would say that the careful handling of the pick, preferably in private, does more good than using a brush, since the former gets the food out of the crevices and cavities, while the latter may only drive it into them. Certainly the Elizabethans, whose dentistry was limited to the services of a tooth-pulling barber, were well accustomed to the pains of what Shakespeare called a ' pugging tooth '.

Those who wish to discredit Stratford and the Shakespeares never omit to mention that in 1552, twelve years before the birth of the boy William, his father, together with two of his neighbours, was fined a shilling for leaving a dung-hill in their street. It was not a sanitary age and London, which began to substitute the water-closet for the earth-closet forty years later, was not much better than Stratford. At least in Stratford the dung-hill was made a cause of punishment and was not accepted as a normal nuisance. The fine probably led to better ways.

But while the Elizabethans were careless about creating bad smells, they did their best to remedy the nasty result by much sprinkling of herbs and flowers in their houses. Their gardens were used for growing useful herbs as well as flowers and fruit, and these were put to healthy purposes. It is obvious that Shakespeare, especially in his latter days when he was once more a Stratford resident, was not only fond of flowers but a keen observer and student of gardening. His description of flowers is ample and exact, as well as enthusiastic.

Sir Francis Bacon's famous essay ' Of Gardens ' shows the amount of care and labour which was devoted to lawns and flower-beds by the owners of great houses. He listed at length the blossoms obtainable in the various months, aiming at ' perpetual spring ' by discreet planning of the planting. He laid down a scheme for a garden of some thirty acres including ' a heath or desert ' as well as flower-beds, fruit trees, alleys, hedges, aviaries, and fountains. He was opposed to pools for sanitary reasons, and he was particularly eager that the air should be continually scented. Lavender was popular for this reason.

So we can see the country town and country life of the time in fair perspective. There was good, if harsh, schooling. There was literacy and a fair supply of books to read. There was a wide range of sports and games. There were regular visits by troops of players of which more will be said later. In a place of Stratford's size an intelligent and active boy could grow up with plenty to see and to enjoy, even if he found the hours of instruction long and the discipline applied to 'a breeching scholar in the schools' severe. There was always the escape, and Shakespeare has himself described the happiness of that, not only in the phrase 'as willingly as e'er I came from school', but also in some lines in *Henry IV*, Part· 2 :

> My lord, our army is dispers'd already :
> Like youthful steers unyok'd, they take their courses
> East, west, north, south ; or, like a school broke-up,
> Each hurries to his home and sporting-place.

There is a double Stratford memory here, of the beasts freed from labour and of the youngsters now at liberty to seek the games of their choice.

CHAPTER THREE

Catering and Cures

CATES, from which word we get our caterers and catering, were to the Elizabethans the more elegant and costlier forms of food. Other articles of diet, e.g., cheese and garlic, could be tasty, but they were not cates. Shakespeare contrasted a meal of cheese and garlic with feeding upon cates. Hamlet said that God providently catered for the sparrow, implying, if not a rich menu, at least a sublime sauce. The derivation of cates seems not to be an abbreviation of delicates and delicacies but a shortened English form of the French verb *acheter* ' to buy '. Cates were shop-goods, not the produce of a man's own farm or garden. To Shakespeare oranges and lemons would be cates and apples would not.

During his lifetime, England, with its growing skill and daring in navigation and its far-flung voyages, east and west, was beginning rapidly to widen its catering. The fruits imported from afar were coveted and the alien spices were much employed in cookery. But country towns and districts, like Shakespeare's Stratford and Warwickshire, were compelled to be mainly self-sufficient in their food-supply. It is difficult for us to imagine the isolation of the English countryside when the nation's internal transport was so closely restricted by the scarcity and roughness of the roads. Indeed, England under the Romans probably had better communications than England under the Tudors.

The slow motion of the few carriers' carts, the menace of bandits, and the bumpiness of the rural tracks in dry weather and their soddenness after rain made long-distance transport of

loads of food almost impossible. So the countryman, especially
in the centre of England, lived on his meat and still more meat.
London could get fresh sea-fish brought by boat right up the
Thames : but the areas not close to harbours would have only
limited quantities of salted fish and would depend for their change
from meat and for their Lenten fare on catches in their own
streams and ponds, of which carp was the most esteemed.

Agricultural scene

The flesh of the cattle, sheep, and pigs had to be eaten in a salted
form during the winter and spring. The business of feeding stock
through the months when the native pasture had no nourishment
was particularly difficult when big root-crops were hardly known
and there was no imported ' cake ' to eke out the supplies of local
hay. The hay itself might fail in a wet season when the grass went
mouldy in the fields. Shakespeare in *A Midsummer Night's Dream*
alluded to one most disastrous summer, probably that of 1594.

65

The rivers overflowed and swamped the meadows.

> . . . the winds, piping to us in vain,
> As in revenge, have suck'd up from the sea
> Contagious fogs ; which falling in the land,
> Hath every pelting river made so proud,
> That they have overborne their continents :
> The ox hath therefore stretch'd his yoke in vain,
> The ploughman lost his sweat, and the green corn
> Hath rotted ere his youth attain'd a beard ;
> The fold stands empty in the drowned field,
> And crows are fatted with the murrion[1] flock ; . . . .

It was not always plenty in the Avon Valley, especially when the Avon was bursting its banks. Even in the best of years, when Michaelmas came and the grass ceased to be its rich self, it was necessary to keep only the breeding stock through the winter : the farmers had to kill the rest for salting. A diet of salt meat is not a healthy one, as the sailors discovered : they took limes to ward off the scurvy caused by deficiency of vitamins. (Not that they knew anything about vitamins, but experiment and experience had taught them to take fruit and vegetables whenever they could.) Apart from stored apples and nuts, the native fruits of England do not outlast their season and there was no canning industry to add big supplies to private bottling. Consequently the common disease of Shakespeare's countryside, as we know from the records of his medical son-in-law, Dr John Hall of Stratford, was scurvy.

There was a great difference between town and country feeding. London had its oranges and lemons ; London also had wines in abundance, but wine was heavy stuff to carry by land. The banquets in London strike us as prodigious in the number of dishes.

---

[1] Murrion meant both a cattle-disease and the flesh of beasts killed by the disease.

But when Mr Justice Shallow entertained Falstaff and his followers in Gloucestershire, the supper was, by Tudor standards, simple. ' Some pigeons, Davy, a couple of short-legged hens, a joint of mutton, and any pretty little tiny kickshaws, tell William cook.' (Kickshaws, an adaptation of the French *quelques choses*, were sweet dishes.) There was dessert later, pippins with caraway seeds.

This menu seems lavish to us who have experienced rationing by government and must also continually be rationed by high prices and heavily taxed incomes. But contrast it with this bill of fare for a dinner (midday) advocated for a good housewife in 1587 :

The First Course

Potage or stewed broth, boiled meat or stewed meat, chickens and bacon, powdered beef, pies, goose, pig, roasted beef, roasted veal, custard.

' Sirrah, go hire me twenty cunning cooks '—*Romeo and Juliet*

The Second Course

Roasted lamb, roasted capon, roasted chickens, peahens, baked venison, tart.

Similar repasts were outlined for supper. All this cannot have been eaten at once. Presumably the vast array of dishes were there for choice and there were many servants to finish them after. It is noticeable that these lists make no reference to vegetables. There were not the masses of starchy potatoes with which modern families fill up the gaps. The Tudor world had just discovered what they called Virginia potatoes, but these were regarded as a luxury and were enormously expensive.

The country people depended much on pigeons, which are not so much mentioned in London banquets. To have a dovecote or pigeon-house was the right of the Lord of the Manor : the peasantry were forbidden to breed pigeons, because too many of these birds caused havoc among the crops. The great dovecotes can still be seen by us (mainly in disuse) beside the old Tudor country houses. There was a particularly impressive one at Kinwarton not far from Wilmcote, the family house of Shakespeare's mother, which also has its dovecote. At Kinwarton this building was seventy-five feet in circumference and twenty-five feet in diameter and had six hundred nesting holes. The product of such a huge pigeon-colony could feed a family through many winter meals. But not everybody likes pigeon meat even at rare intervals. Taken in mass, it is said to be unhealthy. There is even an old tradition that a man who eats pigeon for thirty days in succession will die !

It has been pointed out to me by a friend who does his own cooking—and preparing—of meat and poultry that pigeons have no gall-bladders : he added that Shakespeare knew about this, since he makes Hamlet say, while censuring his own reluctance for revenge,

But I am pigeon-liver'd and lack gall
To make oppression bitter.

Pigeons flutter frequently in Shakespeare's texts, but he never mentions them as poisonous in bulk or even as wearisome. After all, when at Stratford, he did not know great variety of feeding and his family would be grateful for the change that pigeons provided.

Where a modern English family, or at least its adult members, would feel the greatest loss, if we had to return to an Elizabethan diet, would be in the complete absence of coffee and tea. To start the day without either would be intolerable to most of us, and we are further accustomed to ' elevenses ' and to tea in mid-afternoon. Many people take even more cups of tea than that. We know that light beer was regarded by the poor as a morning pick-me-up after a night of heavy drinking. Christopher Sly, waking after his debauch, cries ' For God's sake, a pot of ale,' whereupon the servant of the nobleman who has put him in a lordly bed says, ' Will't please your Lordship drink a cup of sack ? ' A cup of sack (what we would call a sweet sherry) would be regarded now as a nauseous potion for the day's beginning.

Perhaps to the gentry then early-morning sack was preferable to the cup of milk with which we have to imagine younger members of the Shakespeare family starting their day, while their father and mother took light ale. Going off to work or school and getting through the long afternoon without a cup of tea would certainly be a dismal prospect to the people of today who take the consoling and stimulating leaf for granted.

Travellers, like Fynes Morison, while relating the extremely carnivorous habits of the English, noted that the Italians ate more vegetables and salads and far more bread. This was natural since rain-swept England has much richer pasture for oxen and sheep

69

than has most of sunnier and more mountainous Italy. Morison took a poor view of this bread-eating, observing that all fullness of the stomach is ill and fullness with bread the worst of such evils. Beef was the staff of life for him. There was general comment by foreigners, as well as by English tourists who could make comparisons, on the quantity of food laid out by the English when entertaining. A table was not thought to be well laid and supplied unless the dishes covered the whole of its surface and were actually standing on one another.

The Queen at a picnic

The day's feeding began with a very early breakfast : but that was not a large spread. Dinner was the midday meal. William Harrison in his *Description of England* (1587) said that the nobility, gentry, and students dined at eleven and took supper from five onwards. Merchants dined at twelve and supped at six. Farmers also dined at noon and, being industrious, worked late in summer and supped about seven or eight. The servants got what was left, which must have been plenty. Harrison added that the English begin with 'the most gross' food and end with the most delicate. The Scots, on the other hand, had a canny alternative to this. Calculating that they might be crammed with the gross dishes before they got to the dainties, thus letting the staff have the latter, they began by polishing off the tasty kickshaws and then, if sated, they left only some of the heavy stuff to the menials.

Fridays were generally observed as fish days, a salutary discipline when there was such steady application to the meat dishes during the week. Queen Elizabeth endeavoured to compel still more consumption of fish, and Wednesdays were commanded to be as meatless as Fridays : it is uncertain how far this ordinance was observed. She was not considering her subjects' health so much as the defence of the realm. To have large fishing-fleets based on the country's harbours was to have ready the far from raw material of a practised and seamanlike navy when occasion came to man the galleons and the guns instead of putting out the nets.

The fish diet was by no means monotonous. We have the food-lists of a bachelor who lived in lodgings in London in 1587. Presumably he was entertaining when his menu contained 'a side of haberdyn (halibut ?)' and another of 'green fish', four plaice, some whiting, and a conger eel. With this went dressed salad, white wine, and claret. His parade of meat dishes on other days was on the usual lavish scale. Was it for himself alone that he ordered a piece of beef, a loin of veal, and two chickens ? He was careful to add fruit, oranges, lemons, and, in June, strawberries and cream.

The banquet in a big house, whether in town or country, was indeed a large matter and had its traditional forms and rankings. The host sat with his family and his close friends at the top table : below them, ' below the salt ', as it has been called, were placed the less important guests and the more important members of the retinue. Later on, and outside, there was often a charitable disposal of the remnants of the feast to the poor who arrived to collect the bits and pieces. These must have been substantial considering the vast array of meats originally served.

It became the fashion during Shakespeare's lifetime not to drink out of the gold and silver cups which the rich families regarded as a normal part of their domestic equipment, but to use instead the fashionable and beautiful glassware which was being abundantly imported from Venice. The wines drunk were mainly European ; during the Middle Ages English squires and clerics, especially in the south and west, had endeavoured to develop their own vine-yards and to provide their own wines ; but what was produced was, owing to the handicap of our less sunny climate, naturally inferior to the vintages of other areas more fortunate in their summers and their ration of sunshine. There was a wide variety of imports from which to choose and the cost was not oppressive. When a Swiss traveller, Thomas Platter of Basle, visited England in 1599, he and his companions were entertained by the Lord Mayor of London, and he has recounted the scope of the hospitality in the very interesting record of his journey which gives us many sidelights on Shakespeare's England.

Along with the copious dishes served the guests were offered the best beer together with a range of heavy and light wines to follow. Platter specified Greek, Spanish, Malmsey (from the Azores), Languedoc, and other French and German vintages.

He did not think that the Lord Mayor would be ruined by such hospitality : in England, he said, all kinds of wine could be had comparatively cheaply because of the low cost of carriage by sea. But, as has been pointed out, as soon as land-carriage over any distance had to be arranged, the difficulties and expense of supply were much increased. London was fortunate then, as always, in the convenience of its river and harbour for international trade, and the Elizabethan Londoners were regular consumers of many other European wares in addition to the wines.

One would think that the results of such lavish drinking might have been stupefying. Platter tells us that the Lord Mayor's midday dinner and subsequent hospitalities lasted until evening : after that the guests were accompanied home—it is possible that they needed some help and guidance. But Harrison says that it was regarded as a breach of manners both to be over-talkative at banquets and to drink too much. Those who became what he called ' cup-shotten ' did so from carelessness or inexperience of such festivities. If they exceeded the limit, they were penitent afterwards, regarding it as no small disgrace to have lost control of their speech or limbs.

There had been ale of various kinds in England for a long time, but a strong beer made of malt and hops was an invention or importation of Shakespeare's own century. A writer during the reign of Henry VIII described it as ' a natural drink for a Dutch-man ' and added that it was much consumed in England to the detriment of many Englishmen. There was a rhyme which said :

> Turkeys, carps, hops, pickerel, and beer
> Came into England all in one year.

The year was somewhere about 1530. (Pickerel were young pike-fish. The word turkey for the domesticated wild-fowl first appears in English writings in 1555.)

Fynes Morison said that our soldiers who fought in the Netherlands learned some drinking habits from the Germans and brought home the custom of large '*garaussing*' (carousing). The earliest form of carouse was the emptying of a mug at one draught. In *Hamlet* Shakespeare attributed to the Danes a gross delight in 'heavy-headed revel', but that passage was tactfully omitted from a later edition of the play printed when the Queen of England was Anne of Denmark. Her husband, James I, passed a law for the punishment of drunkards, but his own Court was by no means innocent of excessive drinking, as we know from an account of a Royal Masque at which the lordly dancers and performers were incapable of keeping on their feet and the entertainment collapsed in shameful confusion. Shakespeare introduced plenty of topers into his plays and put into the part of his fat knight, Sir John Falstaff, a most eloquent praise of the quickening powers of sack which, in the speaker's opinion, stimulated the brain as well as bestowing courage. It is significant of the desire to put the blame elsewhere that bravery attained by drinking has been called Dutch Courage by the English.

But the exploitation of drunkenness for purposes of comedy, as in the case of Falstaff, does not mean that the author justified the soaking of a carouse. In the tragedy of *Othello* Cassio's reckless drinking leads to fatal results and it is Cassio who says, 'O God ! that men should put an enemy in their mouths to steal away their brains ; that we should with joy, pleasance, revel, and applause transform ourselves into beasts.' This may well have been Shakespeare's own sentiments on the subject, for there was a chance remark made by John Aubrey to the effect that Shakespeare was not a party-goer, excused himself from too festive occasions, and 'would not be debauched'. When we remember the amount of work that he did as actor and in management of a company of players as well as in his prolific authorship, it is unlikely that he can have risked dulling his energies and wasting his nights with ' heavy-headed revel '.

He wrote in a more kindly way of country festivities than of urban indulgences. There is a particularly attractive picture of simple and genial hospitality in *The Winter's Tale*. This sounds like a personal reminiscence of a hostess in some Warwickshire farmhouse. A shepherd is speaking :

> . . . when my old wife lived, upon
> This day she was both pantler, butler, cook ;
> Both dame and servant ; welcom'd all ; serv'd all,
> Would sing her song and dance her turn ; now here,
> At upper end o' the table, now i' the middle ;
> On his shoulder, and his ; her face o' fire
> With labour, and the thing she took to quench it,
> She would to each one sip.

The ways of eating and drinking in Tudor England were not conducive to long sustenance of health : the young, able to take vigorous exercise, could shake off the results of a plethora of meats and of a good thirst killed by kindness. But when life became more sedentary the heaviness and monotony of the feeding was a handicap to longevity.

Shakespeare himself reached the age of fifty-two and so did his actor-colleague, Richard Burbage. But of his fellow authors a number died quite young and that through illness and not because of war, civil disaster, or execution for one of the many crimes, from treason downwards, which involved the death penalty. (The death-rate among public men was accelerated by the gallows and the block.) His co-operators in play-writing for his own company, Beaumont and Fletcher, died at forty-six and thirty-two respectively. Among his rivals we need not count the fiery and eloquent Christopher Marlowe, because his death at twenty-nine was caused by a tavern-brawl. Robert Greene died at thirty-four, Thomas Nashe at thirty-four, and George Peele at thirty-eight. These three were poets and playwrights, of the type known as University Wits, since they had, unlike Shakespeare, enjoyed the advantage of a college education, Peele having been entered at Christ Church in Oxford and the two latter at St John's in Cambridge. The writers, with a limited market and low prices for their work, had a hard struggle financially in London and probably suffered from irregular as well as ill-chosen meals and from the solace of hard drinking when they had money to indulge in liquor.

In families the death of children was not regarded as exceptional and tragical: a certain number of casualties would be taken for granted. Shakespeare himself was one of eight; only his sister Joan lived longer than he did and of his three other sisters two died in infancy and one at eight. His brothers lived to be forty-nine, forty-six, and twenty-seven. Shakespeare's only son, Hamnet, died at eleven. A family which had such a succession of funerals would be regarded as exceptionally unfortunate today, and the family doctor would not be regarded as having done well by his patients.

The main affliction of the age was the recurrence of bubonic plague which swept the country and still more the cities with appalling devastation. Shakespeare himself was lucky to escape it soon after his birth. *Hic incipit pestis* (Here begins the pest) was written by the Vicar, John Bretchgirdle, on 11 July 1564, in the Stratford Register when recording the burial of a boy. The casualty list beside the Avon of that summer and autumn was indeed heavy: between January and mid-July the parish church had twenty-two burials; between mid-July and the end of the year there were two hundred and thirty-seven. This means that more than an eighth of the town's population was wiped out.

Mary Arden's house at Wilmcote

Those who could left the town, and we may owe the continued existence and so the plays and poems of William Shakespeare to some such escape. His mother, who had already lost her first two children from one cause or another, could go to her family home at Wilmcote and possibly did. But it is known that his father, as Borough Chamberlain, stayed in Stratford to cope with the town's problems as well as to maintain his own business. There was another epidemic of plague at Stratford in 1597 ; but on this occasion the casualties were much fewer.

In London, plague was a constant menace and a frequent and a fearsome fact. It was a double pest to the writers, since their livelihoods as well as their lives were in danger. The theatres and all places of entertainment were closed by order to prevent spread of the contagion. The actors were put out of work and had to go on tour. There was a long visitation of the plague in 1593, when Shakespeare was just achieving success : he seems to have used the time profitably by getting on with the composition of plays for future production and by writing his narrative poem *Venus and Adonis*. This had a great reception, sold well when it was published in the following year, and established Shakespeare's name. There was another outbreak soon after the accession of King James in 1603. At St Saviour's (now Southwark Cathedral), the Bankside Church nearest to the riverside theatres where Shakespeare worked, there were six hundred and twenty burials in August of that year and seven hundred and thirty-five in September. It has been estimated that thirty thousand deaths from plague occurred in London within a year.

The authorities did what they could to mitigate these disasters, but of course the conditions of life were conducive to an unchecked spreading of infection. The scavenging of the city was largely left to the kites and crows, and the garbage bred flies by the million in hot weather. The water-supply was dependent on local and easily contaminated wells. Drainage hardly existed. Medical knowledge was elementary by our standards. Scented herbs were used to purify the air in the streets and homes, but these were a quite inadequate form of safeguard. Plague houses were isolated and sealed up and swift burial of the victims ordered. But, without more medical science and without the efficacious drugs and disinfectants which we have today, the battle was hopeless : the horror had to work itself out and time had to be the slow healer of London's wounds.

In the plague year of 1603 the playwright and pamphleteer Dekker wrote a terrifying description of the London scene when plague was rampant. Here is a glimpse of the public panic and

Maid brushing away flies

'Afflicted with these
strange flies'
Romeo and Juliet

distress. (But it must be remembered that Dekker usually wrote, as they say, 'at the top of his voice'. He was a dramatist as well as a recorder.)

What an unmatchable torment were it for a man to be barred up every night in a vast silent charnel house, hung (to make it more hideous) with lamps dimly and slowly burning in hollow and glimmering corners : where all the pavement should, instead of green rushes, be strewed with blasted rosemary, withered hyacinths, fatal cypress and yew, thickly mingled with heaps of dead men's bones : the bare ribs of a father that begat him lying there ; here the chapless, hollow skull of a mother that bore him ; round about him a thousand corpses, some standing bolt upright in their knotted winding-sheets, others half mouldered in rotten coffins that should suddenly yawn wide open, filling his nostrils with noisome stench and his eyes with the sight of nothing but crawling worms.

79

. . . He that durst in the dead hour of gloomy midnight have been so valiant as to have walked through the still and melancholy streets, what think you should have been his music ? Surely the loud groans of raving, sick men, the struggling pangs of souls departing ; in every house grief striking up an alarum ; servants crying out for masters, wives for husbands, parents for children, children for their mothers ; here he should have met with some frantically running to knock up sextons ; there, others fearfully sweating with coffins to steal forth dead bodies lest the fatal handwriting of death should seal up their doors. And to make this dismal consort more full, round about him bells heavily tolling in one place and ringing out in another. The dreadfulness of such an hour is unutterable.

This was the other side of the medallion that was Merry England. It was the atmosphere in which some of Shakespeare's greatest work, especially in tragedy, was written. Small wonder that he made frequent reference to the ' passing-bell ' and ' the surly, sullen bell ' which were the constant and all too solemn music of English towns in times of epidemic.

One of the most haunting and poignant of Elizabethan poems was written by Thomas Nashe during the plague of 1593. It is called *In Time of Pestilence*. Here are two of the stanzas.

Rich men, trust not in wealth,
Gold cannot buy you health :
Physic himself must fade ;
All things to end are made ;
The plague full swift goes by ;
I am sick, I must die—
　　Lord, have mercy on us !

Beauty is but a flower
Which wrinkles will devour ;
Brightness falls from the air ;
Queens have died young and fair ;

Dust hath closed Helen's eye ;
I am sick, I must die—
Lord, have mercy on us !

Less lethal than the plague, but none the less a serious affliction and sometimes a killer, was ague. Ague is defined as a malarial fever, with paroxysms, having three stages, cold, hot, and sweating. There are frequent allusions to agues and ' sweating fevers ' in the plays ; the wretched sanitation and the puddles in the undrained streets were a fertile breeding-ground for insects who would themselves be fertile breeders of disease. It is significant that Bacon in his essay ' Of Gardens ' warns his readers against having standing water : ' pools mar all and make the gardens unwholesome and full of flies and frogs.' He had the ague in mind.

There is a passage in Shakespeare's play *King John* describing the imagined death of a young boy. Queen Constance of France has grim forebodings about the fate of her son, Arthur of Brittany. The passage seems to be written with intense personal feeling : since it was written about the time when Shakespeare lost his own and only son Hamnet (August, 1596) it may well have been inspired by that bitter loss. In it occur the lines :

And he will look as hollow as a ghost,
As dim and meagre as an ague's fit. . . .

The allusion to ague and the weakened, emaciated body can at least suggest to us that it was this disease which caused the bereavement in Shakespeare's home.

Considering the diet, it is not surprising that Shakespeare mentioned indigestion and heartburn. But the chief product of a monotonous meat diet was scurvy, and the medical records of his son-in-law, Dr John Hall, which the latter wrote out in Latin, frequently mention this malady and its treatment with an apozeme, which was an infusion of herbs. This prescription of plant juices was a sensible policy and provided the patients with some of the missing vitamin C. Hall related the sufferings of a Lady Underhill who was attacked by intense irritation of the skin 'as it were biting of ants in many parts of her body'. The apozeme in her case was most effective, curing her 'as if it wrought by enchantments'. But some of the doctor's other salves sound more sinister than enchanting. One of his poultice prescriptions, as Dr Martin Mitchell has stated in his book on *The Shakespeare Circle*, included 'swallow's nests, dirt, dung and all, boiled in oil of chamomel and lilies'. To this was added the faeces of a dog and hen's grease as well as sundry herbs, the whole, of course, to be applied hot. One can imagine that almost any malady would be preferable to such a remedy. Yet Dr Hall was highly esteemed in the Midlands and had as his patients the region's aristocracy.

There was, as always, quackery, but the respected Tudor doctors, who were then often called Medicines, were for the most part men internationally trained. There were Royal Professors of Medicine in the universities of Oxford and Cambridge after 1546. In London there was an established College of Physicians and a Company of Barber-Surgeons ; intending physicians usually included medical courses at foreign universities and took foreign degrees. (Dr Hall had studied in France.) The most famous doctor of Shakespeare's time was William Harvey who went to Italy and became an M.D. of Padua University. In 1616, six days before Shakespeare died, he delivered an epoch-making lecture to the College of Physicians in which he expounded the doctrine of the circulation of the blood through the heart, arteries, and veins. That the blood flowed about the body had been known ; and Shakespeare shows acquaintance with the idea. Harvey demonstrated its passages exactly and destroyed the theory that the heart was only a fountain of supply.

But, despite erudition at the top of the profession, and a careful study of anatomy by the surgeons, there was much crudity in the treatment of diseases and of course antiseptics were unknown. Dentistry consisted of tooth-pulling in which the barber was supposed to be proficient. There must have been many a foul-smelling mouth in the best of Elizabethan company ; Shakespeare alludes chiefly to the rank odour of the multitude, but Bacon in his Essay ' Of Masques and Triumphs ' advises the injection of scent, ' Some sweet odours, suddenly coming forth without any drops falling ', as a wise defence against the ' steam and heat ' of fashionable revels.

It was not only the poor who could taint the air with their presence. Andrew Boorde, who wrote what he called a *Dyetary of Helth* in 1542, advised that a fire be lit in the bedroom in the morning not only for warmth's sake but also to ' waste and consume the evil vapours within the chamber '. He counselled closing all windows, especially those of the bedroom, at night ; he hopefully believed that ' the breath of man may purify the air within a chamber '. Though rich people had curtains drawn round their four-posters, they were advised to wear thick scarlet night-caps and ' go to bed with mirth '. Boorde was a great believer in merriment as an aid to sleep : he wisely did not expect anyone to start the day laughing : coughing and spitting were to be the first exercise of the morning. He said nothing of the daily bath. Hands, face and teeth were to be washed in cold water.

It is sometimes said that we now, at least in Britain, are too fond of open windows and that we are so obsessed with daily bathing that we do injury to our skins by washing away the natural fats. However that may be, we manage to live longer than did the Elizabethans who did not overwork their limited water-supplies by constant turning of taps for bodily use. Their consumption of meat and drink was likely to produce high blood pressure. This was dealt with by frequent cupping and the laying on of leeches ; the other evil results of indulgence at table were

Left : Dr Hall's Dispensary,

and below : Hall's Croft

treated with induced vomiting and with purging by rhubarb and senna (both mentioned by Shakespeare), and by other potent drugs. In the administration of these Dr Hall was an enthusiastic practitioner. He made a squire who had taken a surfeit of cream at the end of a large meal vomit ten times, ' which answered desire ', and he cured, as he claimed, a dropsical countess by giving her eighteen and fifteen motions on successive days together with further sweatings and purgings. If the pleasures of the table were strenuously pursued, they were also strenuously paid for.

At the same time we must admit that Shakespeare was much more polite about doctors than he was about lawyers and schoolmasters. Cerimon, in *Pericles*, a play which he re-drafted and strengthened with some typically splendid passages, claims that his knowledge of

> the blest infusions
> That dwell in vegetives, metals, stones ;

had enabled cures which gave him

> A more content in course of true delight
> Than to be thirsty after tottering honour,
> Or tie my treasure up in silken bags,
> To please the fool and death.

Thereupon one attending on him praises him as Lord Cerimon whose cures are numbered by the hundred and whose financial generosity is boundless.

Dr John Hall had come to Stratford-upon-Avon about 1600 ; he was Shakespeare's near neighbour and married his daughter, Susanna, in 1607. *Pericles* is generally dated at 1608. We may surmise that Hall had made a good impression, despite some of his medical methods, and had won very kindly opinions for his profession.

CHAPTER FOUR

By Road and Water

WHEN Shakespeare travelled from Stratford to London for the first time he may have been in the company of players who had recruited him for their service or he may have gone alone, seeking enlistment. In either case he may have had to walk it : if in luck, he rode. A third possibility was a place in a carrier's cart, but the carriers did not go often and they had chances of more profitable loads than human passengers with very little money to pay for their fare. There was no possibility of going by coach. The roads were too rough for bowling along in a four-in-hand. Royalty and the very rich could travel in some state. No such amenity existed for the general public.

Shakespeare could have made the journey to London by either of two routes. He could have climbed up over Edgehill, later on the scene of the first battle in the Civil War, dropped down into Banbury, and then gone on through Bicester and Aylesbury : or he may have preferred the route by way of Oxford and High Wycombe. The motorist of today has the same choice and, whichever way he prefers, he will not be lonely. Solitude was the dread and peril of the Elizabethan traveller : now it is the empty road that we seek.

There are old anecdotes which link Shakespeare with places on both these itineraries. The gossiping writer John Aubrey (1626–1697) has told us that the poet ' happened to take the humour of Dogberry at Grendon in Bucks which is the road from London to Stratford '. Dogberry, the comic constable in *Much Ado About*

Nothing, a character who anticipated Sheridan's Mrs Malaprop by his muddling of words—it was he and not Mrs Malaprop, who said that comparisons are odorous—may well have had his prototype in an English village ; the scene of the play is Italian, but the name of Dogberry has more ring of Bucks than of Messina. Grendon lies just off the present main road between Bicester and Aylesbury, and Shakespeare could have made it one of his stopping-places if on one occasion he had found the company congenial. But the lodging there would not be luxurious.

Aubrey also recounts that Shakespeare, going into Warwickshire once a year, commonly lay at the Crown Tavern in Oxford. The landlord of the Crown was the father of Sir John D'Avenant (1606–1668), the future Poet Laureate and an active author and manager when the London theatres were reopened after the Restoration. D'Avenant used to boast that he himself was Shakespeare's son and that the hospitality at the Crown had something to do with that. However that may be and whichever road the traveller preferred (he may well have used both as the mood seized him), the journey would be slow and hard. Compared with the general level of civilities and amenities in Elizabethan life, the methods of transport were slow, crude, and comfortless. The roads of England were in a far worse condition than when the Romans were laying them down nearly fifteen hundred years earlier. Here, in the development of communications, was one of the notable failures in human progress to which allusion was made in the first chapter.

We have plenty of contemporary evidence about the shocking inadequacy of the roads. Fynes Morison (1566–1630) was a Cambridge scholar who made extensive journeys across Europe as well as across England. His accounts of the social conditions that he met are most valuable. He stated that the roads outside London were so foul that coaches could use them for only one or two days' drive in any direction from the capital. Near the city they were kept fair and sanded, a task involving continual labour. To hire a coach was extremely expensive and beyond the reach of any but the great. A good meal at the common table of an inn cost only fourpence or sixpence, but a coach with two horses cost ten shillings a day for hire and, if there were three horses, fifteen shillings. So Englishmen, says Morison, rode upon their own horses : if they hired a horse it cost them two shillings the first day and a shilling or one-and-sixpence thereafter ; after that the passenger had either to bring the horse back or to pay for the sending of him and also to arrange for his fodder both going and returning. Shakespeare, as soon as he made money, which did not take him long, would have had his own horse.

O happy horse to bear the weight of Antony !
Do bravely, horse ! for wott'st thou whom thou movest !

One is tempted to quote this cry of Shakespeare's Cleopatra, substituting William for Antony. That horse was carrying a cargo without which the history of the English theatre and of English literature would have been infinitely smaller.

There were carriers with covered waggons who took passengers as well as goods from city to city, but Morison says that this method of travel was so tedious, since the driver of this jogging conveyance left one inn so early and stopped at the next so late, that none but women and people of inferior condition or foreigners used to make use of such transport. (His reference to women is scarcely chivalrous.) So most men rode, in company if they could find it, not only to relieve loneliness but as a safeguard against the numerous thieves and robbers. Accordingly the riders went well armed with daggers and pistols. If Shakespeare carried home his London gains for the support of his family in Stratford, he must have seen to it that he had stout companions and have tried to avoid night-travel, gaining shelter from the highwaymen before dark.

The west yet glimmers with some streaks of day :
Now spurs the lated traveller apace
To gain the timely inn.

Shakespeare gave those lines to the First Murderer in *Macbeth*. The criminal classes knew about their victims' fears.

For Government business and for other important messages and news there was a service of speedy ' post-horses '. (From their gallopings the word ' to post ' came to mean to make all haste.) But the normal rider had no change of mount and so was used to taking things in a leisurely manner, proceeding twenty or thirty miles a day, according to the state of his horse, of the roads, and of the weather. Since Stratford is about a hundred miles from the centre of London, the journey may have taken Shakespeare as much as four days with three nights to be spent at inns on the road.

Morison speaks well of the inns where the servants ' hoping for a small reward in the morning' were readily attentive to man and beast. The traveller of means was not compelled to share the four-penny or sixpenny ' ordinary ' at the public table. He could feed *à la carte* and be served in his own room. There would be musicians to play for him if required. Such service must have been available only in the larger hostelries in the larger places : Shakespeare would have music, no doubt, in the Crown at Oxford, but not in a village tavern, like that at Grendon. The man who preferred solitude and a selected meal in one of the better inns would be charged five or six shillings for his supper and breakfast and he would also give a few pence to the chamberlain and ostler. Other recorders of English journeys pay tribute to cleanliness and good furnishing, describing the scenting of parlours, bed-chambers, and privies with sweet-smelling herbs and flowers.

One danger, which Shakespeare has himself described in *Henry IV*, Part 1, was the corruption of the chamberlains and the inn servants by highwaymen, who would pay for information about the arrivals, departures, and whereabouts of travellers likely to be worth the robbing. When Falstaff is out with his ' minions of the moon ' and ready to show his prowess as a thief on the road, his party is told by the chamberlain of the inn at Rochester that a franklin (a free-holder of land) is at large in the wilds of Kent with three hundred marks of gold on his person. For this the informer is offered a share in the plunder.

It is unlikely that all the inns were of the quality that Morison described. Plagues of insects and vermin were certainly one of the risks of the traveller. Allardyce Nicoll, in his volume of extracts from writers of the period, called *The Elizabethans*, includes under the section on ' Roads and Inns ' the observations made by one Thomas Hill in 1581 on the various ways of killing fleas. The fleas must have been extremely numerous and active in order to justify the amount of labour and medicaments needed to combat them, if Hill's advice were taken. The traveller, in his view, should anoint his staff with the grease of a fox or hedgehog ; this would gather all the fleas to that feast and so avert them from his own person. He was also counselled to ' fill a dish with goat's blood and set the same by the bed and all the fleas will come to it roundabout. Also take the fat of a goat and anoint what you list therewith.' There were other and less messy preventives of attack. It was suggested that beans boiled in water with wormwood would make a liquor which, sprinkled about the room, would do good defensive work. Several other herbs are named as helpful. But the last suggestion about fleas is at least the simplest. ' Taking them between your nails you may bruise them at your pleasure.'

The landlord of an inn that was a flea-pit could hardly have kept all these remedies in stock, since that would have been a confession of filthy premises. But if the wayfarer had to carry his own outfit of fox grease, goat's grease and goat's blood, together with a supply of beans, wormwood and assorted herbs, he must have added some troublesome items to his luggage.

Concerning the hostelries of the London to which Shakespeare came for the first time and from which he used to return, more prosperous, at holiday intervals—there is a tradition that he did so once a year—we have some good evidence in the records of Dr Thomas Platter of Basle, whose entertainment by the Lord Mayor has already been mentioned. He stayed, in the autumn of 1599, at an inn called ' The Lily ' in Mark Lane in the City ; there he was at the centre of things and had no great distances to travel on his sight-seeing, which included the theatres and bear-pits as well as the Guildhall and Westminster. Since he returned to the Lily after his excursion to Oxford, he must have been well satisfied with its service.

The town that he encountered was throbbing and humming with entertainment. To the Lily came musicians and drolls for the pleasure of the guests. Platter noticed that the numerous London inns and beer-gardens were usually well provided with sports and diversions. These places, he said, were eagerly and frequently visited by women as well as by the men of·the town : the ladies thought it a considerable treat to be taken to such centres of meeting and conversation where they were refreshed with wine sweetened with sugar. At the inns there was much smoking of tobacco, but Platter does not say whether the women carried their own pipes with them.

In our time tobacco is suspected of causing cancer of the lung, and, whether or not that be true, it is generally considered to be a drug that is unlikely to do one's health any good, however much it may soothe the nerves. But Elizabethans actually regarded it as a health-giver in addition to being what we now call a 'tranquilliser'. Gerard, who wrote a treatise on herbs, praised tobacco's disinfectant

91

and curative qualities and Platter alludes to it as a medicine as well as noticing its provision of merriment and agreeable drowsiness. After smoking, a draught of Spanish wine was taken. Many people, however, thought the habit a filthy one and King James I denounced it in the strongest possible terms in a tract called *A Counterblast to Tobacco* (1604).

> And for the vanities committed in this filthy custom, is it not both great vanity and uncleanness, that at the table, a place of respect, of cleanliness, of modesty, men should not be ashamed to sit tossing of tobacco pipes, and puffing of the smoke of tobacco one to another, making the filthy smoke and stink thereof to exhale athwart the dishes, and infect the air, when very often men that abhor it are at their repast ? . . .
>
> Have you not reason then to be ashamed, and to forbear this filthy novelty, so basely grounded, so foolishly received, and so grossly mistaken in the right use thereof ? In your abuse thereof sinning against God, harming yourself both in persons and goods, and raking also thereby the marks and notes of vanity upon you : by the custom thereof making yourselves to be wondered at by all foreign civil nations, and by all strangers that come among you, to be scorned and contemned. A custom loathsome to the eye, hateful to the nose, harmful to the brain, dangerous to the lungs, and in the black stinking fume thereof nearest resembling the horrible Stygian smoke of the pit that is bottomless.

But Thomas Platter, ' a stranger come among you ', raised no objection to the pipe-smoking in the inns ; though he did say that preachers cried out against it and he added as a warning that the inside of one man's veins after death was found to be as thickly smeared with soot as if it were a chimney.

Platter stayed in several places, but he made no complaint of the inns at any of them. He did, however, bear witness to the wretched condition of the roads in the country. He was able to get about fairly well in nearby excursions from the Lily in Mark Lane. He and his party drove by coach through the borough of Tooting to visit the royal palace of Nonsuch at Cheam. This he described as ten or twelve miles from London, an isolated building with not a house in its neighbourhood : it had a deer-park, magnificent gardens with topiary, i.e., trees and bushes cut to imitate the shapes of animals, etc. It was a Sunday, and he saw the Queen at a church

The Queen arriving at Nonsuch Palace

service. On the way back he stayed at an inn in Kingston. The journey was comfortable. Later he took a drive to Richmond Palace, where he himself enjoyed a game in the tennis-court, and this excursion also was easy and quiet.

But, outside London, he ran into great difficulties. It was possible to drive to Oxford, by way of Windsor and Wycombe, and his coachman had agreed to make a round trip (at sixteen shillings a day) which would bring him back to London by way of Cambridge. But at Oxford the driver raised objections : he said that the cross-country road to Cambridge was marshy after recent rain and hard to trace through the sodden land. Moreover, the journey would mean going through desolate country with the

Travellers passing Windsor Castle

ugly chance of exposure to highwaymen. He had hired his coach at a great cost from a nobleman and already it had a damaged wheel. He dared not risk being bogged down in some remote part of the midlands. That would be ruin for him.

Platter actually appealed to the Chancellor of the University, which could hardly happen today, since neither the Chancellor nor the Vice-Chancellor of a university is now concerned with the troubles of tourists : they have other and loftier matters in mind. The appeal led to an examination by the best carriage-builders and menders available, and the verdict was that there would be many hindrances on the road to Cambridge and that to attempt the drive would be much too dangerous. The coach could, however, with adequate repair on the spot, get safely back to London including a deviation to Woodstock, which place Platter wished to see. The Chancellor, whose word seems to have been law over citizens as well as students in Oxford, ordered the coachman, under severe penalty, to take Platter to Woodstock and so back to the capital. This was safely reached by way of Wycombe and Beaconsfield, whose broad street, still so agreeable to the eye, was noted with favour by the Swiss traveller.

If Platter had made that journey to Cambridge, one of the robbers who might have sent him home a poorer man was the notorious Gamaliel Ratsey. This rogue was the terror of East Anglia at the time. He was caught and hanged at Bedford in 1605 after a life of humorous, as well as profitable, raids on the travelling public. He is said to have conformed to the romantic ideal of a land-pirate by wearing a hideous mask as well as being well-mounted and a brilliant horseman. After his execution an anonymous booklet was published called *Ratsey's Ghost*, in which anecdotes of his life were collected.

One of these stories told of his meeting with a troupe of players at an inn. He paid them forty shillings for a much-enjoyed performance, which was double what they were taking on tour ; on the following day he made up for this liberality by pursuing them and forcibly relieving them of the fee which he had just paid. Ratsey must have had his associates, or the players must have been very poorly protected against such attack : a whole troupe would hardly have yielded to one man, however terrifying his masquerade.

The robber, however, though he took the money, was ready to give advice in exchange, telling the troupe to keep to London in future. He thought they could flourish there since one of them was excellent in his performance and the second-best Hamlet of his acquaintance. The reference to Hamlet suggests that this was the play with which his victims were touring.

If the best performance of Hamlet in Ratsey's estimation was that of Richard Burbage, the company whom he had tricked was unlikely to have been Shakespeare's ; but his further allusion to successful and prosperous players who took country houses can be regarded as a hit at Shakespeare's acquisition of New Place in Stratford. Ratsey's talk with the players can be interpreted in several ways ; what matters is the light which the affair throws on the conditions of journeying in shires not far from the capital. Platter's apprehensive coachman had good reason for his fears.

In London itself the streets were mainly narrow and crowded. Because there was a fair enough surface for wheeled traffic, the wealthy folk could use carriages, and these were of two kinds. The major coaches, used for long travel, could hold a family party ; the smaller vehicles, called caroches, carried one or two passengers. The difference between the two types of conveyance resembled that between the old four-wheeler and the two-wheeled hansom of Victorian and Edwardian London. But the coaches and caroches were privately owned or only hired on contract, as Platter hired for his excursions : there was no regular supply of what we call cabs for getting about town. It must be remembered that the distances to be crossed were not big and that walking to the river-side from north and south would not involve much expense of time and energy. The transport from the west to the east of London was mainly carried on by water : the Thames was amply supplied with craft called wherries as well as with the barges of royal and noble owners. In fact, the river was the thoroughfare in which carriage of people and goods was chiefly conducted.

Dekker has left a vivid picture of the noise and tumult in the London streets, but allowance must be once more made for his love of dramatising the scene. We think of London today as a place oppressively obstructed with a dense and deafening stream of traffic. But Shakespeare's London, as Dekker saw it, had its own nuisance of crowding and of din. He described not only the clatter of sweating porters and water-carriers but the merchants, shopkeepers, and craftsmen bustling about as though they were playing at leap-frog or dancing a measure. The wheeled traffic of the professional carters and of the rich men's coaches made, in his opinion, a thundering racket, while ' at every corner men, women, and children meet in such shoals that posts are set up of purpose to strengthen the houses lest with jostling one another they should shoulder them down '. We have our own occasional accidents and even disasters caused by over-crowding of enthusiasts at popular gatherings for sporting events or at regal spectacles, but at least we do not expect the mobs to knock down houses in addition to knocking each other over or about.

There was only one bridge to link London with its southern suburbs and the road to the Kentish ports : it was therefore of supreme importance. There had been a road-crossing of kinds for·centuries, with bitter struggles for its possession, which might lead to pillage of the city.

> London Bridge is broken down,
> Gold is won and bright renown

was a war-song before William the Conqueror came. In Shakespeare's time London Bridge was a massive viaduct, with a road running between substantial houses and shops built on either side of it. Platter described its twenty arches and these finely built homes of prosperous merchants set upon it. He also mentioned the tall stakes to which were then affixed more than twenty skulls of noblemen who had been executed for treason or other capital offences. This kind of display, revolting to us, had long been on view, and Scots will read with disgust that the head of their patriot hero, William Wallace, was exhibited there early in the fourteenth century, while the quarters of his corpse were sent for exhibition in Newcastle upon Tyne, Berwick, Stirling, and Perth. The people of London were used to this parade of skulls from which the birds of prey had plucked the flesh long ago, and Shakespeare, whether he walked or took a ferry from his lodgings to the Globe Theatre in Southwark, must have been well accustomed to this decoration of the London sky.

The practice of skull-showing on the bridge continued for some sixty years after his death : the heads of the regicides were placed there after the return of Charles II and the overthrow of the Parlia-

3

mentary leaders. Platter observed that it was a matter of family pride among Londoners to claim that an ancestor's skull had been honoured with a place in this grisly mixture of open-air mortuary and museum, since the nobility were the usual occupants. But commoners could get a place there too. Jack Cade who led the popular revolt in 1450, which is given lively treatment in the second part of the play of *Henry VI*, qualified, after his defeat and execution, for a position on the bridge.

The piers of the bridge were protected by wooden platforms called starlings and these further obstructions naturally made the passages for the river-flow very narrow: hence the pressure of water going past was severe, leading to a rapid downpour through the arches and to considerable danger in navigation. Those concerned with their own safety insisted that the boatman cross from north to south well above or below the danger-area, but some of the boatmen liked to show off by shooting the rapids and so proving their skill. But the skill was not always sufficient and there were constant and fatal catastrophes.

In 1582 an ingenious Dutchman was allowed to attach a water-mill to the bridge and thus exploit the power inherent in the rushing stream. It made a clashing noise and was famous for its contribution to the general uproar of London life. A character in a play by Shakespeare's later colleagues, Beaumont and Fletcher, likened a vociferous woman to the noise of London Bridge.

Along the banks clustered the boatmen with their wherries, clamouring for passengers who wished to cross to and from the numerous landing-stages on either side or to use the river for transport up and down stream. (Hence the cries of 'Eastward Ho' and 'Westward Ho', which continually rang out across the water.) Platter described the busy commerce of the crowds of boatmen seeking to get customers and shouting about the superior comfort of their own vessels. He stressed the protective awnings, the elegant upholstery, and the comfort of the seats in the wherries and was delighted with this kind of London transport.

The river did, indeed, provide one of the town's main industries. The boatmen had a vigorous spokesman and quite an accomplished writer at the beginning of the seventeenth century in John Taylor, known as 'The Water-Poet'. He stated that two thousand small boats were to be found about London in his time, and that along the whole reach of the river from maritime Gravesend away up to Windsor there were forty thousand men earning their living with oar and scull. The watermen had to have a licence to carry on their business and they were subject to fixed prices : the regular fee for a crossing of the river was a penny and up to sixpence could be charged for longer journeys east and west. This was a bitter grievance in the eyes of the boatmen who said that the cost of living kept rising while their fees had been regulated fifty years ago. (Down the centuries the cost of living nearly always rose and still rises : the demand for higher wages to meet higher prices is almost eternal.) So the oarsmen demanded tips and were renowned for their flow of bad language if those tips were absent or inadequate. Their ranks were filled with naval veterans who had sailed against the Armada or on the great voyages to the Indies ; these sea-dogs were regarded as some of London's toughest characters and famous for their ' unreverend speech '.

It was fortunate for the wherry-men that the principal places of entertainment, whether providing the gory spectacles of the cockpit and bear-baiting or the gentler arts of the theatre, began to be clustered on the South Bank. Since the majority of the patrons of these entertainments lived north of the river, they provided the necessary custom. It was estimated that three or four thousand people crossed the Thames daily to visit the theatres in Southwark.

It was, of course, a precarious living for the watermen since a hard winter would interfere with attendance at theatres open to the sky, while an epidemic of plague would close them altogether. There was a vehement protest made by the riverside workers when it was proposed to build another theatre in north London. This, it was said, was 'unfair to the wherrymen' and would mean hunger in Southwark. That the number of boatmen living in that suburb was very big is shown by a list of baptisms in the parish church. The parents included seventy watermen compared with only ten of various other occupations.

On a fine day the Thames, then really the High Street of London, must have provided a splendid spectacle. There stood London Bridge, with its architecture as well as its utility. Streaming across the water were not only the boats plying for public hire but also the large and elegant barges used by the Queen, the Court, and the men of wealth and title. Between Whitehall and the City the nobles owned great houses with splendid situations on the North Bank. These faced over the river towards the sun and were graced with their own water-gates leading down to their private jetties. The names of London's streets in this area are still reminiscent of these mansions and their owners. The title of the Strand explains itself. Norfolk, Essex, and Arundel Streets proclaim the old town-houses of the territorial barons. The Savoy area was once the home of John of Gaunt, but it was badly burned during the rebellion of Wat Tyler in 1381. Somerset House changed hands frequently and it changed its name too for a while, when James I gave it to his Queen, Anne of Denmark, and named it Denmark House.

There were melancholy aspects of this traffic as when a man condemned for treason—a charge of wide application—was brought up the river from Westminster to the Tower of London and landed at Traitor's Gate, which can still be seen. Again, lower down stream at the Execution Dock of Wapping, pirates and water-thieves were hanged at the low-tide mark. The executioner there might decorate the horrid scene with the unusual privilege of his crimson breeches, but the view was not improved by the bodies of his victims which were left until three tides had overflowed them. To this sight Shakespeare alluded in *The Tempest* when Antonio, cursing the boatswain as a rascal, cries

> Would'st thou might lie drowning
> The washing of three tides !

So the Thames, with the skulls on the bridge as well as its sodden corpses on the jetty-steps, was also London's Sinister Street as well as its principal and most handsome thoroughfare.

Swans brought their curious grace and flash of white to its waters, sometimes riding placidly, sometimes in trouble. Shakespeare had noticed one

> With bootless labour swim against the tide
> And spend her strength with over-matching waves.

Fishing went briskly on. Salmon came up the still-unpolluted Thames to spawn far away in the farther reaches of the stream. Platter said that many salmon and sturgeon were caught with rod and line in London River. It was easy then for a stroller to find water-meadows instead of the endless docks, warehouses, and suburbs of today. Shakespeare's contemporary, Spenser, the Poet Laureate, describes how he

> . . . Walk'd forth to ease my pain
> Along the shore of silver-streaming Thames ;
> Whose rutty bank, the which his river hems,
> Was painted all with variable flowers,
> And all the meads adorn'd with dainty gems
> Fit to deck maidens' bowers,
> And crown their paramours
> Against the bridal day, which is not long :
> > Sweet Thames ! run softly, till I end my song.

It was ' silver Thames ' to the Tudor poets and silvery it still can be, but only under the very bright sky of a radiant day. Moreover, it rang with melody and song : it was customary for the passengers in the barges and the wherries to bring their musical instruments with them and to add to the pleasures of a voyage by playing on their lutes or by chanting glees and madrigals. The wits and gallants of the Inns of Court, who frequently crossed to Southwark for their pleasures, were rivals with their voices. Londoners then were accustomed to music wherever they went.

The national ear seems to have been keen : it was deemed essential to a proper life to be able to take one's part in a round of song. The standard was high. Shakespeare himself often expressed his disgust at a jarring note and a harmony broken. So people who made dismal and distressing noises by singing or playing out of tune would soon have been suppressed by those who knew, and could do, better.

Wherever we turn in a survey of the Elizabethan scene we find strange contradictions. To foreign visitors the country roads seemed to be scandalously bad, but the inns, especially in the larger towns, won their praise. In London itself the stranger was simultaneously impressed by the appalling cruelties to man and beast and by the devotion to beauty in sound, speech, and spectacle. It was as though the traveller's inseparable companions must be gross savagery and high civility, riding together by his side, as it were Caliban with Ariel on the pillion-seat.

CHAPTER FIVE

London Town

I F Shakespeare came to London before the year 1588, as is probable, he was in the capital at a time of peril, glory, and great
political events. A land-war against the Spanish power had
been fought in ' the cockpit of Europe ', the Low Countries. It
had brought some radiance to the rising star of the young Earl of
Essex, who was making a dashing invasion of public life ; it had
cost the life of Sir Philip Sidney ; it had not deterred King Philip
of Spain from believing that he could overwhelm England at sea.
The great Armada was massed for action ; in the middle of July
it was seen off the Cornish coast, a formidable array of nearly one
hundred and fifty ships, needing only expert seamanship to destroy
the lighter English fleet.

But the prowess in naval warfare lay with the English Admirals,
Drake and Howard, and their well-trained crews. Using their speed
to full advantage they harried the Spaniards as they sailed up the
Channel, chased them with fire-ships out of Calais, and finally
drove them on their long, tempestuous, and fatal voyage to the
north. The galleons that had escaped the English guns were soon
doomed to sink, even as far away as the coasts of Scotland and
Ireland. The belief is still held that Spanish gold from a ship's
pay-chest may be profitably fished out of the sea off Tobermory
in the Isle of Mull, one of the inner isles of Scotland's Hebrides.
The diving which is intermittently and optimistically renewed at
Tobermory is a curious link with Shakespeare's England.

The Spanish war was to continue in a desultory way, but with
Spain on the defensive and with the English fleet as a raider which

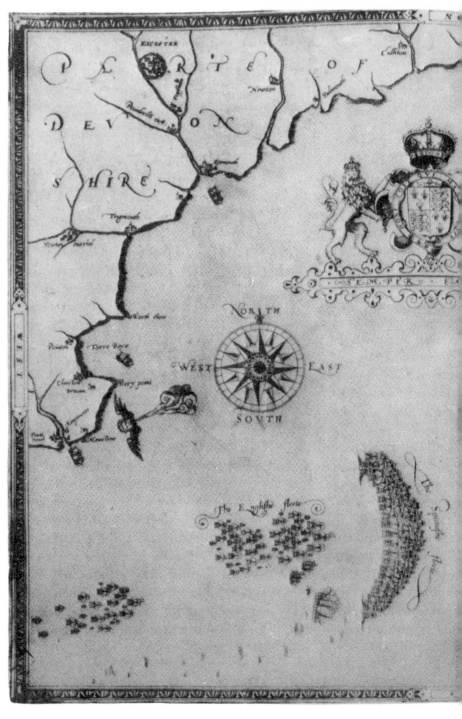

Map showing progress of the Spanish

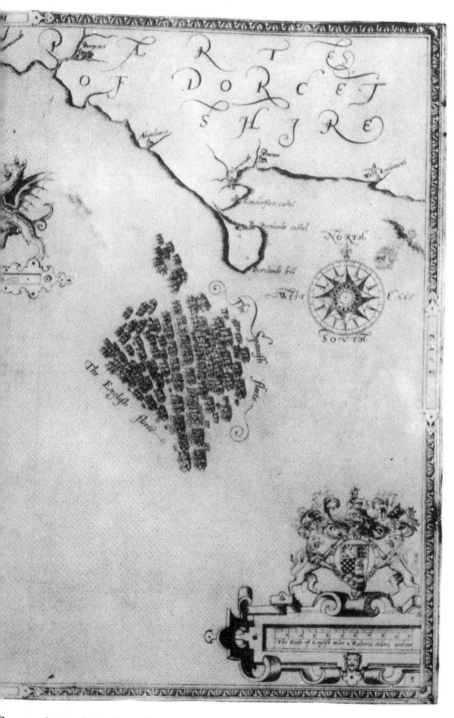

P A R T E

O F   D O R S E T S H I R E

Bridport

Abbotsbury

Waymouth

Wey

Weteneworth

Sandesfote castel

Portlande castel

Portlande bill

The Spanish fleete

The English fleete

NORTH

WEST   EAST

SOUTH

EAST

The Scale of English miles · Roberto Adam · auctore

...leet up the English Channel in 1588

might triumphantly descend on a Spanish port, as it did at Cadiz in 1596. But such escapades, satisfactory to English pride, could not do more than enrage and humiliate the enemy. The King of Spain's beard might be singed : his head remained on his shoulders and his crown remained on his head. But England itself had been released from the great menace which had set the pessimists nodding gloomily about the likelihood of disasters to come in 1588. The prophetic aspects of astrology were seriously regarded and the expectation of total eclipses of the sun and moon caused general apprehension. But in Shakespeare's words, which some think were written early enough to refer to this occasion, the sad augurs mocked their own presage. The year 1588 turned out to be one of delivery and celebration.

But while England could rejoice in a new sense of national

1 August 1588

We whose names are herunder written have determyned and agreede in counsaile to folowe and pursue the Spanishe fleete untill we have cleared oure owne coaste and broughte the frithe [1] weste of us   And then to returne backe againe aswell to revictuall oure ships which stand in extreme scarsitie as alsoe to guard and defend our owne coaste at home with further protestatione that if oure wantis of victualles and munitione were suppliede we wold ~~suppl~~ pursue them to the furthest that they durste have gone

Howard	George Cumbréland
Howard	Edmond Sheffeyld
Fra: Drake	Edw. Hoby
John Haukins	
Thomas ffenner	

Endorsed : 1° August. Determyned by the consayle to returne from thwarting of the frythe

[1] Firth of Forth

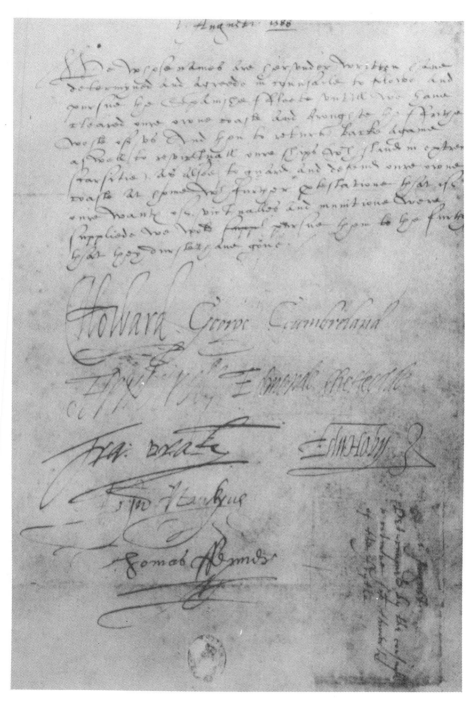

Signatures of the Admirals of the English Fleet which destroyed
the Armada (transcription on facing page)

Phineas Pett,
Master
Shipbuilder
of the Navy

' And why such daily cast of brazen cannon
And foreign mart for implements of war,
Why such impress of ship-wrights whose sore task
Does not divide the Sunday from the week ? '—*Hamlet*

security, it must not be thought that the Elizabethan age offered
security to individuals. We in our time have lived through terrible
dangers of recent war and are living through terrible apprehension
of what war may do, should it come again ; but our statesmen
do not conduct their business with the heads of their predecessors
falling on the block and later suspended on London Bridge ' to
encourage the others '. Our kings do not sign death-warrants for
their wives or our queens for their cousins. Men of high position
do not find themselves whisked hurriedly into gaol because of
some misdemeanour or intrigue with a lady at Court. To hold
rigidly to a religious faith might also be a cause of ruin. The

streets of London might be paved with gold for merchants and with a modicum of silver for young men, like Shakespeare, who had brave words and notions to sell. But they offered a very slippery pavement to those who were seeking careers in politics and affairs of state, or who wished to be 'the observed of all observers' at a court where the Queen was indeed a jealous goddess. She did not, like her successor, publicly propound an assertion of the Divine Right of Monarchs, but she had no great regard for the civic rights of lords and ladies, not to mention mere commoners. Cautious at one moment, capricious the next, she was in her friendships as dangerous as she was powerful, lavishing favours and ruin with dazzling inconstancy.

The Armada year marked important changes of position in the collapsible seats of the mighty. Robert Dudley, Earl of Leicester, an early recipient of the Queen's patronage and for long a power around rather than behind the throne, had been in and out of favour; he was re-established, but he died soon after the rout of the Spanish fleet, at which time he had been Lieutenant General of the army and so responsible for home defence had the Armada justified King Philip's hopes. He had been the grand seigneur of Kenilworth Castle, close to Stratford-upon-Avon, where Shakespeare as a boy may have witnessed the pageantry and heard the water-music when he entertained the Queen with aquatic displays as well as with pomp and revel of all kinds.

Into Leicester's elegant shoes walked his step-son, Robert Devereux, Earl of Essex: it had been thought that Elizabeth might marry Leicester, a man one year her senior. Could it be imagined that she was so fascinated by the far younger man as to see in him a lover, if not a husband? She was obviously susceptible to his looks and gallantry and wrote a love-poem about 'fair Venus' son, that proud victorious boy', which confessed her feelings and her inability to get him out of her mind.

Of her old counsellors there remained the Earl of Burleigh, but he was ageing and his dominant post of Secretary—the word secretary then meant one who was trusted with essential secrets—was being kept for his clever, crippled son, Robert Cecil, then twenty-seven years of age. Among the new men arriving on the perilous fringe of power were Sir Walter Raleigh, who was thirty-six at the time of the Armada, a figure at once alluring and aloof, noted for his 'damnable pride', handsome, brilliant, gifted, and fatally tactless. The Earl of Southampton, now twenty-five, a friend of Essex and a patron of Shakespeare, was also a man who could go far, if he cared to : he had the recklessness of the age and nearly lost his life along with Essex in 1601 after the crazy conspiracy against the Queen. In the background was Francis Bacon, aged twenty-seven, exceptionally able as lawyer and philosopher but less gifted in the conduct of a career. He encountered the jealousy of the Cecils, lacked the wealth of the other aristocrats, and was elbowed out of political power ; but later he took the full course of legal honours, finally becoming Lord Chancellor in 1618.

The temper and especially the insecurity of the times can best be understood by seeing what became of these men. James Shirley, known as the last of the Elizabethan dramatists, wrote in a famous lyric :

> The glories of our blood and state
> Are shadows, not substantial things ;
> There is no armour against Fate ;
> Death lays his icy hand on kings.

The gleam of the headsman's axe was always flashing in the minds of men—and women too. But it was an accustomed glitter : the players of the power-game knew and took their risks. If it be true of Elizabethan London that it had music in the air, there was also a death-rattle in the climate of existence. Expectation of long life was futile, not only because of plague, pestilence, and inadequate doctoring, but because those who took a chance in this dynastic and political gaming-house were putting their lives, as well as their fortunes, on the table. Their luck was sure, at some time, to prove lethal.

The Queen's mother, Anne Boleyn, had been beheaded by order of her father when Elizabeth was a tiny child. If it be true that what children need is a sense of security, she was denied any knowledge of that necessary blessing. During her girlhood she was imprisoned and released and alternately regarded as an heir to the throne and an illegitimate outcast. When she succeeded to the crown she lived long in fear of her cousin Mary, Queen of Scots, the heir to the English throne and the repository of Catholic, anti-Elizabethan hopes. England would be Mary's if Elizabeth declined to marry. That refusal she made ; but she had dealt finally with the Marian menace shortly before the Armada. In February of 1587 Elizabeth signed Mary's death-warrant for conspiracy. It was a dreadful moment for the Queen of England who, apart from any personal feelings, had no relish for seeing a head once crowned now parted from its neck. But it was the rule of the game. As Anne Boleyn, so Mary, Queen of Scots was taken. Death laid its icy hand on kings—and queens. There was no respect of a supposedly weaker sex : in any case ' weaker sex ' is not a phrase which made sense at the Court of Queen Elizabeth.

Of the men already mentioned two went to the block, Essex and Raleigh, the former beheaded with some justice by warrant of Elizabeth and the latter, with no justice, by order of James I. Southampton went to the Tower for his share in the Essex Revolt. (He had already tasted imprisonment for a marriage of which the Queen disapproved.) Bacon, when Lord Verulam and Lord Chancellor, was found guilty of taking bribes and, rather luckily escaping prison, was stripped of all his offices. Once more the glory of high position in the state was a shadow. Shirley had added :

> Sceptre and crown
> Must tumble down
> And in the dust be equal made
> With the poor crookèd scythe and spade.

But the poor were scarcely more secure. The number of capital offences was very great and the number of offenders great in proportion. The axe was mainly reserved for treason in high quarters and beheading on Tower Hill might be deemed an honour due to rank. The rope was for the common malefactors who had not gone far enough or fast enough in out-running the constable, a feat which cannot have been very difficult considering the amateurish nature of the Watch. The gibbet also awaited those heretics who had gone too far in the eyes of the orthodox.

The fate of the Roman Catholics who had broken the law seems outrageous to those of us who have the luck to live in a tolerant community. But in the previous reign the persecution of the Protestants with fire, as well as with the rope, had set a repulsive precedent which it was not in human nature to forget. Man has not ceased to be an avenging animal, and it was an age with small admission of Shakespeare's noble saying, through the lips of Prospero in *The Tempest*, that ' the rarer action is in virtue than in vengeance '. Old horrors were replaced by new. Bacon wrote that ' revenge is a kind of wild justice ', adding that ' the more man's nature runs to it, the more ought law to weed it out.' But in this matter the law did as much planting as hoeing. Judicial process could be used as an avenger and the chances of a fair trial for a prisoner charged with treason were inconsiderable.

The rack was on the premises and statements extracted by it, or by the threat of it, were taken as good evidence by the prosecution : the extraction of ' confessions ' went on in Tudor England as it does under an iron dictatorship today. We have to remember that the Queen's life was always in danger and also that she had been excommunicated by the Pope in a decree of 1570: this meant that it was no sin, in the view of Rome, for an English Catholic to be actively disloyal to the English Crown. Many Catholics remained loyal Englishmen and fought against Spain. But there was always the fear, justified probably by conspiracies in Elizabeth's time, and justified beyond doubt by the Gunpowder Plot in the reign of her successor, that behind the priest lurked the assassin and the traitor.

Murder was no rarity and the contemporary descriptions of London life are explicit about the number and variety of thieves and pick-pockets, as well as highwaymen, ready to exploit the absence of an efficient police force. When Shakespeare entered or left the centre of London by the Oxford road he passed by Tyburn, which was the headquarters of the hangmen. The hard-worked gibbets stood where the Marble Arch now marks the entry to the north-eastern corner of Hyde Park. There was plentiful hanging. The condemned were driven to Tyburn from the various prisons in an open cart with the rope round their necks. This provided a popular spectacle. Then they were 'turned off'. That is to say, the cart was driven from under the gallows to which the rope had been attached. Death was not usually immediate and the friends of the victims, or any merciful spectators, ran in to pull down the feet of the dangling body so that 'the drop' might be made quickly effective.

In the case of heinous crimes the hanging was followed by the disgusting spectacle of drawing (disembowelling) and quartering the body. That was the fate in 1594 of a Portuguese Jew called Lopez, even though he had been a well-trusted doctor and chief physician of the Queen. He was involved, probably unjustly, in a charge of treasonable conspiracy. According to Platter, on each

113

day when the law-courts were sitting twenty or thirty persons were sent to the gallows. There was a cemetery adjacent to Tyburn and the grave-diggers were kept busy. A further manifestation of the law in action was the public flogging of convicted women : this took place outside the Bridewell prison near Blackfriars and the river. Against such free public spectacles had the players to compete.

The savageries of Elizabethan justice seem to have been taken for granted. Platter made no comment on the hangings and scourgings that he reported. ' The sanctity of human life ' was a phrase which had little meaning. If a person chose ' to stick his neck out ', as we say of those who take risks, he knew what to expect. But the ferocity of the supposed deterrent failed to deter. The doomed went, as a rule, unconcernedly, or even with a jest, to the gibbet. In *Measure for Measure* Shakespeare describes one Barnardine, a drunken criminal condemned to death and permitted, since the law had some clemency in this matter of alcoholic consolation, to remain drunk in his cell. The Provost of the City (Vienna) thus describes him :

> A man that apprehends death no more dreadfully but as a drunken sleep ; careless, reckless, and fearless of what's past, present, or to come ; insensible of mortality, and desperately mortal.

When told that the rogue needs advice the Provost replies.

> He will hear none. He had evermore hath the liberty of the prison : give him leave to escape hence, he would not : drunk many times a day, if not many days entirely drunk. We have very oft awaked him, as if to carry him to execution, and show'd him a seeming warrant for it : it hath not moved him at all.

Confronted with his execution, Barnardine replies that he ' cannot consent to die today ', because he is in no condition to make a proper end.

Shakespeare's gaolers are jesters. In *Cymbeline* the warder of the condemned Posthumus advises him humorously of ' the charity of a penny cord ', since it pays all debts and is the great discharger of obligations. ' He that sleeps feels not the toothache.' This fellow could wish that all men were good but that would be ' desolation of gaolers and gallowses. I speak against my present profit.' While the Barnardines of London went drunk to Tyburn, being allowed liquor on the way, the noblemen on their passage to the headsman's block made a point of being elegantly dressed, of accepting the consolation of religion rather than of liquor, of displaying the utmost fortitude, and even of dying with a flourish, a phrase, or a formal speech. When, after his futile rebellion of 1601, the Earl of Essex went to meet the axe in the Tower, he wore under a black doublet an elegant scarlet waistcoat which made a vivid glow, as of blood-red life, when he flung aside his cloak and offered his neck to the headsman and his spirit to the Lord. Before that he had spoken at length, denying that he had ever intended any violence to the Queen, but asking God's eternal Majesty for the pardon of 'this last, this great, this crying, this bloody, this infectious sin '.

If our taste is offended by the sanguinary scenes in the tragic plays of the period, the piles of corpses in Act V and even the displays of mutilated bodies, we must visualise the way of life amid which those plays were written. Reality was melodrama then. It seems curious and odious to us that even in one of Shakespeare's finest tragedies, that of *Macbeth*, the end should come with the victorious Macduff, avenger of Macbeth's murderous misrule and champion of morality, brandishing or displaying on a pike the head of the defeated king, and saluting the new monarch with this ghastly trophy.

> Hail, king ! For so thou art : behold where stands
> Th' usurper's cursed head.

In *Cymbeline*, a romantic play laced with much exquisite and tender poetry and enriched with the enchanting character of the faithful Imogen, the head of the oafish scoundrel Cloten is cut off and displayed, and Imogen has to handle the limbs of the mutilated trunk, thinking that they are those of her husband. Such scenes are a severe embarrassment to modern producers who actually conceal as far as possible the physical horrors. But a supply of calf's blood for pouring over the bodies of the dead, as well as a severed head, were essential 'properties' in the staging of high tragedy in Shakespeare's time. The audiences expected the full ritual of revenge and were not sickened, as we are, by those gory exhibits. After all, they had seen, or could at any time see, 'the real thing' at Tyburn or the Tower.

The drawing of swords and daggers in public disputes and brawls was common in all ranks of society and the players themselves were involved in lethal conflicts. Two of Shakespeare's fellows in the service of the theatre, Ben Jonson and Marlowe, had both been involved in street fights with fatal results and had been on trial and in gaol. When they wrote of fiery action and of bloody deeds, the dramatists brought first-hand experience of the rapier to their use of the pen. Marlowe had luckily dropped out of a three-cornered struggle in which one Bradley, the son of an inn-keeper, was killed by a friend of Marlowe's named Watson. Watson was at length acquitted on the plea of self-defence, but he had spent four months in prison before he received the Queen's pardon. Marlowe was kept some weeks in Newgate Gaol before he was bailed out and finally exonerated.

Ben Jonson's duel was with another player, Gabriel Spencer, who was killed in the affray. Jonson escaped with a brief imprisonment and the branding on his thumb of the letter 'T', signifying Tyburn, home of the gallows. His release was due to his ability to read. One thus literate could plead 'benefit of clergy', clergy being taken in the wide sense of educated persons. The accused man had to read from the Bible to prove that he was one of the ' clerisy ', an old term for scholars. The man who could read his ' neck-verse ', i.e., the lines which kept him from the gibbet, could thus avoid execution after a deadly combat of this kind. Without that favour, London would have lost a future Poet Laureate and one who was often a most popular and successful servant of the theatre.

Shakespeare himself was not, as far as we know, engaged in any duel, but in 1596 a dubious character called Wayte asked for ' sureties of the peace for fear of death ' against a group of people, including Shakespeare and the owner of the Swan Theatre, Francis Langley. But since Wayte was known as a loose weakling dominated by a notorious scoundrel, who was also a Justice, called Gardiner, we may fairly believe that Shakespeare was more sinned against than sinning, and was not proposing or attempting to slaughter the wretched dupe and tool of Justice Gardiner. But these events all drive home to us the fact that all the writers of the time were apt to be fighters too, that they were wise to be schooled in self-defence, and that when they put a duelling scene in their plays they were dealing with affairs of their own, as well as of common, experience. The players, too, would be well trained to put up on the stage a realistic mimicry of the sword-play which they had seen and possibly practised in the streets. When Shakespeare introduced the three-cornered fighting of Mercutio, Tybalt, and Romeo in *Romeo and Juliet*, he may have had memories of Marlowe's share in that sword-play of an angry trio which ended the life of Bradley and caused the double incarceration of Marlowe and Watson.

Crime and punishment were as ugly as abundant, but the roguery had its picturesque and amusing, as well as its macabre, aspects. One of the characters in Shakespeare's early piece *The Comedy of Errors*, coming to the scene of that play, Ephesus, speaks thus :

117

They say this town is full of cozenage ;
As, nimble jugglers that deceive the eye,
Dark-working sorcerers that change the mind,
Soul-killing witches that deform the body,
Disguised cheaters, prating mountebanks,
And many such-like liberties of sin.

The soul-killing witches may have been sinister rather than ludicrous ladies, but one may reasonably suppose that Shakespeare had his own relish of London in mind when he wrote these lines. The mountebanks, selling their wondrous potions and life-giving pills, were a great feature of the street scene, whose multiple humours were copiously set on view in a play of contemporary London and its revels, Ben Jonson's *Bartholomew Fair*. A ramble about town yielded ample matter to the seeing eye, and the ready ear would be equally well catered for in the taverns where the veterans of war on sea or land were famous for their spinning of the yarn with a drink as its reward. To a young man in search of 'humours', as well as of horrors, London was a splendid listening-post.

A typical street scene would include the trading of song sheets, which were readily saleable in a city so fond of music. The dramatist and pamphleteer, Robert Greene, made a special study of 'coney-catching', i.e., snaring of the human rabbit, and in it described the tricks of the ballad monger. 'A roguing mate and such another with him were got upon a stall, singing of ballets.' They drew customers, who fancied the ditties, to pay for copies of them. The accomplices of the singers watched the purchasers and 'noted where every man that bought put up his purse again'. (The people of the period did not as a rule carry their cash loose in their pockets, but used purses, which made matters much easier for the 'nips' as the thieves were called.) Then those who did not buy were warned by the ballad-sellers that there were cut-purses at work so that they too might feel for their purses and betray the whereabouts of their money.

Thus all was well prepared for a raid, which was started by shouldering and thrusting in the crowd, so that 'here one lost his purse, there another had his pocket picked . . . and eight more in the same company found themselves in the like predicament'. The scamps who were running this sly business then pretended to be robbed themselves ; but they could run into trouble. Greene described an occasion when the crowd fell upon and battered the ballad party and managed to drag two of these swindlers before a Justice, and added, 'I doubt not but they had their reward answerable to their deserving, for I hear of their journey westward, but not of their return'. 'Going west', then as now, had a mortal significance : to an Elizabethan it meant the cart ride to Tyburn. That Shakespeare knew this kind of coney-catching is shown by his creation of the knavish ballad-seller Autolycus in *The Winter's Tale*. He practised coney-catching at rustic fairs instead of in the capital, but the method of this 'snapper-up of unconsidered trifles' was somewhat similar to that described by Greene. He pretended to be robbed and then robbed the simple clown who helped him.

This epoch of cruelty, cozenage, and comedy mixed was also an age of foppery and lavish exhibitionism. While many of the Queen's subjects were in rags, not a few were devotees of high fashion. The wealth that was pouring in from the piratical voyages of the English sailors and the wide developments of English commerce was eagerly spent on silks and jewels. The fine gentleman of the day was a desperado in a duel ; he was also a dandy before and after. At one minute he was a hawk, at the next a peacock. He wore rosettes, even gems, upon his shoes when he was not riding booted about his affairs ; he affected especially the starched ruff, which, incidentally, has given London the strange street name of Piccadilly. Another word for the ruff was the peckadil and a prosperous manufacturer and merchant of this article built himself a house close to what is now Piccadilly Circus. This was dubbed by the public Peckadilly Hall. So the title of the place persisted, with the change of a single vowel sound.

Even on the field of battle the popinjay could be seen. The blunt, soldierly Hotspur in *Henry IV*, Part I describes the mincing creature sniffing scent among the victims of the carnage.

> But I remember, when the fight was done,
> When I was dry with rage and extreme toil,
> Breathless and faint, leaning upon my sword,
> Came there a certain lord, neat, and trimly drest,
> Fresh as a bridegroom ; and his chin new reapt
> Show'd like a stubble-land at harvest-home ;
> He was perfumed like a milliner ;
> And 'twixt his finger and his thumb he held
> A pouncet-box,[1] which ever and anon
> He gave his nose, and took't away again.

So the town blazed with colour and its drama of debauchery, roguery, and sudden death was played out on a sumptuously painted stage. The women of wealth outdid the men in the size and splendour of their outfits, in which performance their Queen set an outstanding example of a swollen wardrobe. When she died it was found that she had three thousand dresses ; but this did not justify a charge of personal extravagance—Elizabeth was notably thrifty in many ways—but was occasioned by the royal habit of expecting, and by her obedient subjects' habit of providing, presents of costume. New Year's Day, not Christmas, was then the occasion of seasonal gifts, of which the Queen was a chief beneficiary. At the beginning of 1578 eighty different people gave her new dresses.

The English textile industry produced admirably serviceable

[1] The pouncet-box was a perfume carrier, pierced with holes.

cloths and clothes.   A country renowned for its wool and its weavers yielded 'the honest Kersey' and the frieze with which the humbler citizens were at one time content.   During Elizabeth's reign there was no native production of silk and velvet, which were imported from France and Italy :   the change to domestic manufacture of these luxuries came about 1604 when we hear of them being made by ' Master John Tyce, dwelling near Shoreditch Church, the first Englishman that devised and attained the perfection of making all manner of tufted taffetas, cloth of tissue, wrought velvet,. branched satins, and all other kind of curious silk stuffs.'   For the colours in which they were dyed there were many picturesque names, such as Drake's colour satin, Lady Blush satin, Gosling colour taffeta, Popinjay blue, and Lusty Gallant.

The Puritans scolded the vanity of these attires, but they railed in vain.   The middle-class began to ape the elegance of the lords and ladies :   they imitated the elaborate hats and the silk-tasselled gloves, the intricate dressing of the hair on tires, and the carrying of costly fans.   The lady of fashion had her hair dressed high over the tire, a wire framework often jewelled.   Under this was the rouged cheek.   Facial make-up was widely practised and this was something that seems to have annoyed Shakespeare, who was rarely on the side of the Puritans or averse to elegance.   The vanity of the painted cheek was often on his mind.   ' God has given you one face,' said Hamlet of women, ' and you make yourselves another.' The loveliness of Olivia in *Twelfth Night* was praised because

> 'Tis beauty truly blent, whose red and white
> Nature's own sweet and cunning hand laid on.

But his preference for the simple pink and white of a country girl, ' the queen of cream and curds ', was not popular.   The Queen herself, fighting old age with her enamels, set the pace in defiance of natural pallor and of wrinkles.

Not content with parading finely dressed for the affairs of the day, the notables of both sexes had an insatiable passion for dressing up when evening brought the revels in. At Court and in the halls of the great houses there was constant rehearsal and performing of masques. This mixture of indoor pageantry, dance, and play-acting, was no Elizabethan novelty. The Queen's father had loved these sports and in the play of *Henry VIII* we find this stage-direction : ' Enter King and Others as Masquers, habited like shepherds . . . They choose ladies. The King chooses Anne Bullen.' After the masque, the marriage. Queen Elizabeth had masquing in her blood.

But the simplicity of a shepherd's dress was unusual. The Court Masque, as it grew in splendour and expense, used dramatised versions of classical or mythical themes for which the poets were called on to provide the texts. The productions demanded handsome or bizarre costumes and scenery. They also gave welcome scope to the ladies who wished to display their graces. Courtiers could not indulge their vanity by appearing as actors on the public stage, and no women, whatever their social station, were allowed to work in the theatre with the professional actors. But in a masque in a private house they could strut uninhibited in the miming of a war-like Amazon or glide with the stately elegance of a Greek Goddess.

Bacon's essay ' Of Masques and Triumphs ' affords us a vivid picture of these ' things of great beauty and pleasure '. He studied the technique while he enjoyed the result. The stage-managers of the affair, serving the rich, were able to lay on good lighting. ' The colours,' said Bacon, ' which show best by candle-light are white, carnation, and a kind of sea-water green.' The variety of characters presented in a masque included, along with the feminine beauties, ' fools, satyrs, baboons, wild men, antics, sprites, witches, Ethiops, and pigmies '. After mentioning these exotic roles, Bacon curiously drew the line at ' devils and giants '.

He added a recommendation to hosts : they should be careful to scent the room when such games were afoot. Elizabethan attire made a far from scanty covering and included plentiful padding. In summertime, at a well-attended and energetic masquerade, the heat could well be oppressive and the physical results unpleasant. So Bacon advised that 'Sweet odours, suddenly coming forth, without any drops falling, are, in such a company as there is steam and heat, things of great pleasure and refreshment'.

'Enough of these toys,' was his final comment. (He had to remember the gravity proper to a lawyer and philosopher). But for the dressed-up lords and ladies there was never enough, and the Court of King James soon carried even further and to wildly extravagant lengths the joys of this masquerade. Steam and heat there might be, but there was the natural animation of youth and the added stimulation of wine to quicken the flagging limbs, while the whirl and glitter of the dance were a constant addition to the radiance of the London scene.

There was intense practice of dancing of all kinds. Country festivities set all feet moving. The morris-dancers, wearing 'bells, plumes, and bravery', escorted the May-pole on May Day and were prominent in the Whitsun rites when to 'caper upright as a wild Morisco' was an essential part of the gaiety. The simplest country dance was the Roundel : Titania, in *A Midsummer Night's Dream*, asks for a 'roundel and a fairy song'. More complicated was 'the antic hay' (or hey) which was described as a winding routine : it seems to have made quite a clatter too. The clown Will Kempe says of a girl,

> Yet she thumped it on her way
> With a sportly hey-de-gay.

The Trenchmore was another dance deemed fit for the yokels. Later on, Selden, author of *Table Talk*, deplored the vulgarity of the courtiers who had descended to this kind of prancing. ' In King James's time things were pretty well. But in King Charles's time there has been nothing but Trenchmore and the Cushion Dance, Omnium gatherum, tolly polly, hoite come toite.'

Jig was a general name for any lively step. The jig, given at the end of a play, even of a tragedy, was a farcical sketch with dancing added. A slow, even melancholy measure, was called a dump. Shakespeare in his poem of *Lucrece* spoke of

> Distress like dumps when time is kept with tears.

Many of the dances performed at public revels, such as Sellinger's Round, have been kept alive by the folk-dancers of today.

For the fashionable revels in town there was the popular Galliard with the Cinque-pace as one of its forms. The most stately of the court dances was the Pavane ; more flighty, and demanding great agility, was the Capriole. whose name implies the capering mobility of the goat. Another test of jumping-power was the Volte or Lavolt. In *Henry V* it is mentioned that the English dancing-schools teach ' lavoltas high and swift corantos '. Coranto, as its title shows, was a running dance. Sir Toby Belch in *Twelfth Night* asked Sir Andrew Aguecheek, ' Why dost not thou go to church in a galliard and come home in a coranto ? ' The Lavolt came from Italy, the Allemand from Germany, and the Canary from Spain. Thus a man about town, who wished to shine as a man about the dance floor, had plenty to learn, and all Europe to provide the lessons for a light-foot lad.

There was royal encouragement to dance often and dance well. Defying old age, Queen Elizabeth would set the example, even on Sundays. When there was a report of her lameness she disproved it on the dance floor, and it was said that to get office and patronage at her Court it was advisable to study dancing and to perform efficiently. One of her courtiers, Sir Christopher Hatton, was alleged to have won place, as well as favour, by his excellence in a Galliard.

Outside the halls where the masquing dandies were so ready 'to heel the high lavolt' as well as to wear strange costumes in their amateur theatricals, there were the perils already mentioned. Tudor politics offered a slippery floor on which a fall could be fatal, with Tyburn and the Tower looming in the murky background of the brilliant parade. W. Bridges-Adams, in his excellent history of the English play and its players called *The Irresistible Theatre* wrote, 'It is only on a sunless day that there are no shadows. The Elizabethans exulted in a fierce sun and in shadows black as Tartarus'. Those who could afford to follow fashion and would risk the hazards of a prominent place in the Court of a quick-tempered and capricious Queen, took the shadows with the blaze. They were ready to accept brief life here as their portion, and relieved its insecurity by giving a lavish liberty to their high spirits. Come what may, they liked their existence to be a raree-show in which they could exhibit their own versatility as poets and musicians, as masqueraders, and as partners in the dance.

CHAPTER SIX

Early Stages

THAT was the London to which Shakespeare came. The grave moralists said that it was a sty of sensuality and a parade-ground of false pretences. At the summit of society the nobility could be condemned by the very name of their masquing. Was that not wearing a false face ? They were disguising ; they were playing at ' let's pretend ' ; and that, said the Puritans, was no way for an honest Christian to behave. A good man must be truly himself and shun the sin of make-believe. At a lower level were the players, creatures even worse since they were masquerading all the time and that for money. Sportively and sumptuously the lords and ladies were dressing up as heathen gods and goddesses and dancing like pagans in the mimicry of goblins and sprites ; with more craft and less expenditure the troupes of actors, settled in this Babylon that was London, or driven out by the plague to corrupt the countryside, were also indulging in the wickedness of ' let's pretend '. One day they were the ranting kings and imperial termagants of tragedy ; on the next they were the capering clowns of comedy. But despite the Puritan protests, they found a continually wider and more profitable market : the roofless theatres might be chilly places, but they were warmed with the sunshine of general favour. Court and crowd gave the players increasing welcome.

The Puritans could keep them out of their own stronghold, the City. But elsewhere the evil thing was spreading. The serious, intensely Protestant, citizens believed, as Plato had believed in ancient Athens, that art, in so far as it practised imitation, was practising deceit. That figure, posturing with a tinsel crown on his head, was no king but a cheat. Such falsehood could be infectious and scatter its poison of pretending and deceiving through the foolish and impressionable crowd. Moreover, the mere fact of entertainment meant further hazard : its glamour attracted young people to hear stories in which passion prevailed and the deadly sins were attractively on view. An angry Puritan moralist called Stephen Gosson warned the town that ' plays are the invention of the devil, the offerings of idolatry, the pomp of worldliness, the blossoms of vanity, the roots of apostacy, and the food of iniquity '. The players themselves were in Gosson's opinion ' masters of vice, teachers of wantonness, spurs to impurity, and sons of idleness '. ' So long as they live in this order,' Gosson concluded, ' loathe them.'

But the Queen, her courtiers, and most of her people were not impressed by such calls to hatred and were not to be deflected from their pleasure by tirades which contained more abuse than argument. The pretenders, after all, were the mouthpieces of the poets and this England was in love with poetry. As for their power to corrupt, this was easily out-weighed by their use as national voices speaking with persuasive eloquence for patriotic causes. Their plays, if carefully watched and censored in case of error, taught history in a sound way, upheld the cause of England united, and preached the advantages of a peaceful and orderly life under a strong monarchy. Should they teach otherwise and say the wrong and tactless thing, there were not only censors to admonish them : there were gaols in which the knaves could be impounded until their heads were cooled and their tongues more guarded. So there was no royal command to silence these voices and to suppress the lively art which was bringing a new glory to England and introducing some remarkable new brains and wits to the old exercise of dressing up and showing off.

Thus the drama to which Shakespeare was apprenticed was

regarded not only as amusing and exciting but as serviceable to the State. In that it was continuing its oldest function : for this business of 'let's pretend' had begun as a solemn and a sacred matter. In order to understand the art of the theatre at that time, it is necessary to look back briefly to the origins of drama and its growth through the centuries. Whenever and wherever men have joined together in social groups, whether as primitive tribes or as highly organised nations, we find everywhere the habit of enacting stories by wearing costumes and imitating other people. 'Let's pretend' is the essence of children's play and it has been, and remains, in a wide variety of forms the pleasure of adults too, now watching in their millions the make-believe on the screens of cinemas and television sets as well as on the stage.

But this cult of mimicry has not been merely a source of entertainment and diversion. It has been an important element of religion and a means of communion with the gods. Drama is the Greek word for a thing done, and a theatre is the Greek word for a seeing-place. What was first done and seen was usually a form of divine service. The religions involved were pagan and included the festive celebration of nature's fertility, including man's, which was the source of comedy, along with the pursuit of life after death, from which came tragedy.

Man has always believed that the imitation of an act or process can assist in procuring the achievement of desired results. The primitive farmer, who had moved on from the collection of food by hunting to the growing of food by agriculture, emptied water beside his crop when the weather was too dry ; this was his way of asking heaven to send the necessary and nourishing rain. When the corn had started to sprout he leaped in the air beside his field as a hint to the crop to leap up likewise. The dance is an inherent feature of drama ; it is part of the imitation, an active suggestion to gods and men to keep things moving.

The most striking example of this belief in the value of 'let's pretend' is the miming of a life that is lost and found again, the performance of a death and a resurrection. It was deemed of the utmost value to the tribe that the king-hero, usually regarded as semi-divine if not actually a god, should not be altogether taken away from the people whom he had protected on earth. So to imitate his immortality would be to assist or even to ensure it, and therefore dramatic rites, centred round his grave, were held to be of great social utility. So drama sprang up beside the rock-cut tomb of the Egyptian and other ancient kings. Supplies of food and drink were laid beside the mummified body in order to preserve its vitality and help it on its journey to the other world where, undying, the king-hero would remain, as was hoped, the protector of his people on earth.

One of the world's earliest plays was a huge Egyptian drama in which vast numbers of people took part. It presented the life, death, and re-birth of Osiris, who was the deity of water and therefore, in a hot and dry country, the welcome spirit of fertility and of the life that rises, with the flooding of the Nile, from the parched earth. (The earliest of all religious trinities is that of God, man, and soil.) We think of drama and play-acting, at least in their best-known forms, as beginning with the ancient Greeks. Their tragedies sprang from the dancing and chanting of a chorus and were linked up with the rites celebrated at the tombs of the local champions and heroes, who were expected to live on as immortal guardians of their folk. Dionysus, the god closely associated with the Greek drama, was the counterpart of the Egyptian Osiris. He too died, went below the earth, and, like the crops and the vines, rose again.

Shakespeare is quite likely to have seen in his boyhood the folk play, which was acted with remarkable continuity in England as well as all over Europe almost up to our own time. It flourished

129   10

in the Cotswold country, close to Stratford-upon-Avon. It was performed chiefly at the New Year and in early spring, when the worst of the darkness was over, the ploughman was setting out to turn the earth again, and it was time to think once more of planting and fertility. In Thomas Hardy's novel *The Return of the Native* there is a lively description of a Dorset version of this drama as played by the village mummers in Victorian times. One of the characters in this piece of ' let's pretend ' was always the life-giver, in this case the Doctor who cured a combatant supposed to be dead. The Doctor was the symbol of the Life Force and of the annual victory over winter.

The countrymen, who called themselves Guisers (Disguisers), had this folk play of their own. In the cities something more ambitious grew up. That was the Mystery play, whose title did not refer to anything mysterious but was derived from the Latin *ministerium*, meaning a service. Again religion was the root of the matter. The craftsmen of the towns, organised in their guilds, used to celebrate sacred festivals and holidays by performing dramatised episodes from the Bible : they acted first in the nave of the church itself; later they moved to platforms outside the churches ; then they moved away from holy ground altogether and toured the streets with their movable stages sometimes called pageants. On these stages, as their work developed, they built sections called mansions which provided separate spaces for earth, heaven, hell, and so on. The origin of this kind of production was devotional, but cheerfulness broke in and there was no exclusion of broad comic effects. The men of the guilds naturally chose subjects akin to their own trades and crafts : the story of the Ark, for example, appealed to shipwrights and carpenters.

These episodes were grouped in cycles, the most famous of which were written and performed in York, Wakefield, Chester, and Coventry. The Coventry cycle, which included forty-two episodes, was created during the second half of the fifteenth century, a hundred years before the birth of Shakespeare. It was probably still revived when Shakespeare was a boy, and Coventry is only twenty miles from Stratford. One of the great roaring and ranting parts was the villainous Herod, who ordered the Massacre of the Innocents, and it is worth noting that Shakespeare knew of this role, since he made Hamlet talk of an uproarious actor as out-Heroding Herod.

We have some financial accounts of several of the Mystery play productions, including those of Coventry. The actors received money, but they were not professional in the sense of being whole-timers. Their fees were compensation for what amateur athletes call ' broken time '. Rehearsals were paid for by supply of food and drink. At Coventry, Caiaphas and Herod drew top fees, three shillings and threepence. We do not know how many performances that included. Bridges-Adams points out that at Coventry in 1590 ' a rib of beef cost threepence and a quart of wine twopence : a pint of good beer could be had for a farthing '. So the rewards were not so trifling as they may seem to a modern reader. In this case the part of God was priced at two shillings, and those of the Devil and Judas at eighteenpence. At the first rehearsal in Easter Week eightpence was allowed for ale : this purchased thirty-two pints, but we do not know the number partaking.

There was further expenditure on costumes and staging, for which presumably the public paid in gifts, as when a street-musician passes the hat. There was no industry of entertainment then and these town-players of the guilds, like the rustic guisers, expected no more than some recompense for the time given to the preparations and the performance. Later on, the Mystery plays were replaced by Morality plays. In these the narrative values of the Bible stories were superseded by newly-written work in which the characters were not well-known names but abstractions like Mercy, Justice, Truth, and, set against them, the various sins. These rivals fought for the soul of man. The Morality plays, therefore, had less direct human interest than the previous Bible-story plays. To keep the audience from being bored, pieces called Interludes, not necessarily religious or edifying, were introduced, and from the Interludes there gradually came the theatre as we know it. The drama had left the church for the street, and then the street for the hall of the big house or the inn-yard of the general public, and at last it had its own theatres, specially built for this purpose and charging regular fees for admission.

The way was now open for professionals to enter the theatre, expand its work, and improve its standards. Step by step the old devotional exercise, partly service of God and partly a Holy Day spectacle for the holiday-makers, had been separated from its origins. The drama no longer lived by the voluntary efforts of the farm-workers in the folk play and of the urban guildsmen in the Mysteries : instead it provided a living for players and writers who were to give their whole time to the profitable pleasing of the public.

At the universities there was much unpaid acting of classical and scholarly plays by the students. In *Hamlet* Polonius says that he had been an actor at the university and complacently adds that he had been esteemed a good one. Had he not played Julius Caesar and been killed by Brutus ? The students, when they left the university, now found that what they had done as amateurs they could continue to do as professionals. Most went into callings deemed more respectable ; but those who preferred the risks of a literary and stage career to the routine of the teacher's dais, of the desk in a lawyer's office, or of the stool in a merchant's counting house, could go into this magnetic world of greater freedom. The struggle to get on could be hard and many failed to prosper. But there were considerable rewards, as Shakespeare himself found out.

The Puritans of the City of London caused the building of the new theatres to go on outside their precincts, in districts known as the Liberties. These lay both north and south of the Thames. James Burbage set up a play-house called simply 'The Theatre' in Shoreditch in 1576. Another called 'The Curtain' followed it

'The great Globe itself'—*The Tempest*

133

closely. A different kind of building was the indoor theatre at Blackfriars which was exclusively used by companies of boys such as the children of the Queen's Chapel and other teams of juveniles who had for some time been in favour with the aristocratic public and had lordly patronage. The adult actors long endured strong competition from these much-favoured youngsters.

In the south of London there was rapid theatrical development soon afterwards, first at Newington Butts, named after an archery field and situated a mile from London Bridge. Later came 'The Rose' about 1587 and 'The Swan' about 1595. These play-houses were set close to the river, and were handy for those crossing by boat or by foot over London Bridge to spend an afternoon in the pleasure-grounds of the South Bank. In 1599 was built 'The Globe' which became the most famous of all, since it was the headquarters of the Lord Chamberlain's Men, later the King's Men, of whom Shakespeare was a leader : there most of his later work was produced and some of his earlier revived.

Endless argument has gone on concerning the architecture and the stage-arrangements of these Elizabethan theatres. Roughly, the pattern was a circular or many-sided building with a tower : to it the audience was summoned by the blowing of a trumpet and the flying of a flag when the play was to begin. They could either stand, for a penny, in the unroofed yard around the projecting stage (this section of the audience was known as the groundlings) or they could pay for a seat in the covered galleries of which there were usually three. The gallery prices were twopence or three-pence, and threepence purchased the right of a cushion. There were also 'lord's rooms', equivalent to our boxes, for which more was charged. Platter is one of our authorities for these prices and also for the information that there were intervals. He said that when there was a pause in the play the attendants carried round food and drink. On a day of great calamity one playgoer must have been very glad of these refreshments : when the Globe suffered a disastrous fire in 1613, the spectators and players escaped with their lives ; only one man, it is recorded, ' had his breeches set on fire, that would perhaps have broiled him, if he had not by the benefit of a provident wit, put it out with bottle ale '.

The stage itself stretched well out into the floor-space of the groundlings and much of it was open to the weather : in mid-winter these unroofed theatres would have been very draughty as well as wet, and the play-going season did not therefore extend over the whole year. We hear, however, little complaint about the nuisance of bad conditions. Over some of the stage there was a roof alluded to as the shadow or canopy, to which painted cloths called the heavens might be attached : behind it was a gallery over a small inner-stage. The gallery may have been used for the musicians ; but it could also be employed as part of the scenery, representing the walls of a city or Juliet's balcony or the monument to which Antony's dying body is raised in the tragedy of *Antony and Cleopatra*. The inner stage, curtained off, could be opened to reveal a closet, a cave, or a tomb according to need. On either side of the inner stage were doors for the entry of the players. Behind this were the dressing-rooms of the actors. There was a trap-door in the stage for what are called ' trap effects '.

That gives only a rough idea of the general method of theatre design. The details of the architecture have been constantly disputed and, except for specialists, the debate can easily be tedious. Some scholars write as though there must have been one pattern. But why should there have been only one ? Here was a young, vigorous, developing industry ; the art of the theatre was being rapidly improvised by actively experimental people. It is surely most likely that the theatre-owners and actors kept altering their arrangements and were masters of makeshift. Some would prefer to use the back-stage gallery this way and others that, some would

The Swan Theatre

employ the inner-stage, while others found that this caused complaints from the spectators that they could not see into it. It could therefore be used as an extra tiring-room.

Contemporary illustration is scanty. We should not base too much on the copy of a sketch made from memory by a Dutchman called de Witt, who was in London in 1596 and jotted down the look of the Swan Theatre. He put spectators in the upper stage and his inner stage has no curtained recess but two doors, presumably for the entrances and exits of the players who elsewhere came in more at the side. It is likely that de Witt was working on a rather hazy recollection ; it is impossible to accept his placing of some of the galleries whose sight-lines would have been intolerably bad. Those who paid their twopence or threepence surely did not do so in order to get only an occasional glimpse of the proceedings.

Thomas Dekker in a satirical survey of town manners called *The Gull's Hornbook* (1609) tells us that a stool on the side of the stage could be had for sixpence. He then described the outrageous behaviour of the gallants who sat there : they came in late—a bad habit still prevailing with certain playgoers. After that they would pick rushes from the floor to tickle the ears of their fellow gallants and to make other fools laugh ; they would ' mew at passionate speeches and blare at merry ; find fault with the music, whew at the children's action, and whistle at the songs '. They would smoke and spit and ' presumed to be a guider and stand at the helm to steer the passage of scenes '. Dekker admits that ' the ' scarecrows in the yard ', i.e., the groundlings, hated this kind of wealthy oaf who hindered their pleasure in the play. They would hoot him and hiss him and loudly cry ' Away with the fool '. ' After that,' says Dekker, ' it were madness to tarry.'

How, it may well be asked, could any decent sort of performance be given with all this going on ? Would Shakespeare have endured to write, and his fellows to act, work of any quality if this was really to be the kind of risk it ran ? First it must be remembered that the satirists and recorders of the follies of the time were writing for effect and were prone to exaggerate, describing the extreme offender as though he were normal, in order to make lively reading. Further, the de Witt drawing shows no stools on the stage and, if they were there, they would have been so conspicuous that he would hardly have forgotten them. There are strong tributes to the decent behaviour of the audiences. An Italian visitor, for example, called Busino, who visited London theatres a year after Shakespeare's death, commended the silence and sobriety as well as the elegance of the English audience. Platter described the standing in the yard and the sitting in the gallery but said nothing of stools on the stage or of unruly and unmannerly conduct. We can best assume, from this conflicting evidence, that there were sometimes and in one or other of the theatres, perhaps when business was bad and money much needed, stools on the stage so that crude vulgarians could expensively misuse the privilege of sitting on them. But we can also conclude that this nuisance was not everywhere, or even often, permitted.

The women could not be professional players but they dearly loved going to the play. Platter noticed that ' they have more liberty than in other lands and make good use of it ', going abroad not only to the taverns, as we have seen, but to the theatres. If their Queen was an eager spectator, the rest of her sex could not be kept from these delights. The royal example was a great boon to the players : it helped them both in their fight with the City Puritans and by giving a lead to the female devotees of the drama. Busino noticed that theatres were frequented by many good-looking and well-behaved ladies who took their seats among the men without the slightest hesitation, there to watch boys pretending, probably with a most persuasive skill, to be women.

Of course the enemies of the theatre had to claim that these places became workshops of mischief. Gosson in his *School of Abuse* (1579) denounced the men for ' the heaving and shoving, the itching and shouldering to sit by women '. The latter were provided with pillows for their backs and pippins to eat by those who would win their favour, until all was ' such toying, such smiling, such winking ', that it was a comedy to watch, and by no means the kind of comedy that a good citizen should approve. ' Privy and unmeet contracts ' —' dates ' in the slang of our time—were said to be made by the members of the audience, but we can write off at least some of the Puritan abuse as being part of the routine of their righteousness. Those who are always horrified by their neighbours' behaviour often see what they want to see instead of what is. We must set against the outcry of those so easily outraged the compliments paid by the foreign tourists to the play-house manners of the time. Probably the strict moralists enjoyed their scolding as much as the scolded enjoyed the play.

One thing is certain. The theatre was vastly popular with people of all classes. Ben Jonson described the public whose verdict determined the life or death of plays as

> Compos'd of Gamester, Captain, Knight, Knights' man,
> Lady or Pusill [1] that wears mask or fan,
> Velvet or Taffeta cap, rank'd in the dark
> With the shop's Foreman or some such brave spark.

His allusion to the dark suggests the roofed-in private theatres, of which more will be said. But the low roofs over the seats in the various galleries would keep out a good deal of light during the daytime performance in one of the public theatres that have been described, and thus facilitate the conduct denounced by Gosson.

Even the very poor would scrape up money to go to the theatre. One writer of the time, called Crosse, author of *Virtue's Commonwealth* (1603) said that 'many poor, pinched, needy creatures that live on alms and have scarce neither cloth for their back not food for their belly, yet will make hard shift but they will see a play, let wife and children beg and languish in penury'. Since the public theatres were open only in the afternoons, the working men had either to take time off or wait for a public holiday.

Thus the majority of the audience were, as Nashe explained, ' Gentlemen of the Court, of the Inns of Court, and Captains and

---

[1] Pusill was another spelling of pucelle, a maid.

139

Soldiers about London.' But the unemployed or under-employed, with a groundling's penny in the hand, would flock to a play-house as readily as to a bear-baiting. The apprentices to the various crafts and trades were also keen attenders but sometimes unpopular with the management. They were notorious for rowdiness and even for violent riot, and their massed arrival at the theatre doors would cause apprehension. A house called the Cockpit was wrecked and even set on fire by a mob of these youths in 1617. The wildest and silliest of university 'rags' in our time had their parallel tumults in the outbreaks of the Tudor apprentices.

The so-called private theatres were as old as the public ones. In a hall at Blackfriars the boys of the Chapel Royal—that is to say, those young members of the choir who were eager and able to act as well as sing—had been giving performances since 1576; their companies continued there till 1608, when Shakespeare's fellowship, now the King's Men, took the place over. Blackfriars then became even more important than their public headquarters at the Globe : to have a roof was to have warmth, comfort, the costly but alluring benefits of artificial lighting, and the considerable attraction of being able to give performances at night. It was possible to introduce spectacular effects that could not be achieved on an open stage ; and one can trace the effects of the new conditions on the plays written. Decorative masques, for example, could be introduced with the knowledge that their graces would be well displayed. Moreover the groundlings were not there to be a nuisance. A more discriminating audience was attracted.

Shakespeare had never been contented with the nakedness of the public stages, as he made plain in the speeches of the Chorus in *Henry V*. He described his platform as ' this unworthy scaffold ' and apologised for the inadequacy both of his stage-armies and of the ' wooden O ' in which they were cramped.

Where,—O for pity,—we shall much disgrace,
With four or five most vile and ragged foils,
Right ill disposed, in brawl ridiculous,
The name of Agincourt.

It was surely rather hard on his company and on the man who had
'disposed' the players and arranged the fights to have their efforts
thus dismissed as pitiful and laughable. The lines certainly suggest
that, if Shakespeare had possessed all the resources of a modern
theatre or a film-studio, he would greatly have enjoyed using them.
No doubt, when the time came, he warmly appreciated the superior
amenities of the Blackfriars.

Why then were the public theatres built roofless ? One answer
is that it was very much cheaper to shelter only the galleries and
the back-stage parts than to cover the entire building ; the managers
were thrifty and the players themselves never had much capital to
invest. Candles, too, were a luxury. At Blackfriars more could
be charged for the seats, and the gross receipts were much larger
than at the Globe although the building was quite a small one.
The covered theatre was available at all seasons, which meant a
steady income instead of one liable to interruption by ' winter and
rough weather '.

Acting indoors to the better-mannered and less fractious and
fidgety spectators could be increasingly intimate and delicate.
The theatres constructed after 1600 were usually roofed. The
tradition of the inn-yard had been forgotten : the equivalent
to the private house and the great chamber of the Court or the
lord's mansion was preferred. In Stuart London the move was
towards cover and comfort, in such new constructions as the
Salisbury Court and the Cockpit.

CHAPTER SEVEN

The Play and Production

W E naturally wonder what we would think of a Tudor or Jacobean theatrical production could we be magically privileged to look back and see one. The scenery was probably limited to some painted cloths; necessary chairs and tables could be carried on and off. The inner-stage, if used, would be helpful for 'interiors'. But, in general, the setting was quickly indicated by the dramatist in his text. For instance, when the move is made in *As You Like It* from the Duke's court to the woodlands, Rosalind is quickly given an explanatory line, ' Well, this is the forest of Arden,' and Touchstone immediately follows it, lest there should be any doubt, by adding, ' Ay, now I am in Arden.' When the story moves to the Welsh mountains in *Cymbeline*, the journey to Milford Haven is announced by Imogen in the last line of Act IV, Scene II. Then, when the switch has been made, old Belarius explains that ' we house in the rock'. He says this in order to let the audience know that the inner-stage has become a cave. He follows this with mention of ' yond hill' to suggest the mountains.

The fact that no hill was visible would not dismay the audience. Probably without programmes, they were used to listening attentively for scene-changes. Often the setting was superbly painted in words for their benefit. It may have been in the radiance of a sunny day that the first audience of *Hamlet* trooped into the Globe, a ' world premiere' indeed, though with the world triumph to come quite unsuspected. They would not know, unless they had heard some gossip about the new production, that they were to meet at midnight at Elsinore. But the hour and the Danish nation, the blackness and the cold, are at once made manifest. There could be no lighting-effects or glimpse of mountains far away when

> the morn, in russet mantle clad,
> Walks o'er the dew of yon high eastward hill.

Who cared ? It was all there in the words.

We must assume that for a presentation of this kind the Lord Chamberlain's Men would not allow stools on the stage with the risk that one of Dekker's tiresome characters would come lurching in after too good a lunch and ' mew the passionate speeches ' of the Prince of Denmark. We can surmise too that the Globe, especially for a new venture, collected, in the main, an audience of intelligence and one eager to hear every word that a leading and popular dramatist had to give them. If the play were performed uncut, which is unlikely, they would have heard Hamlet's advice to the actors, which was obviously aimed at the professionals of the time. They were not to ' o'er-step the modesty of nature ', not to split the ears of the groundlings, not to saw the air with their hands, not to strut and bellow, not, if they were playing comedy scenes, to introduce ' gags ' and seek the easy laughs of the shallow listeners and the ' barren spectators '.

This scolding of ham-fisted performance may have been aimed at the rival company led by Alleyn ; but it is so general in its terms that it seems to be Shakespeare's criticism of the general level of acting at the time. It is unlikely, I think, that the lines were then spoken, since it is hardly credible that he would both insult his groundling audience and then invite his fellow-actors to make speeches stressing their own faults to the audience. The censure was put into the text by a playwright with a grievance : when he had written it he had got that off his chest. Another point is that Shakespeare was said, by an old tradition, to have himself

143

Edward Alleyn
' Was accounted a good actor '
Hamlet

appeared as the Ghost of Hamlet's father. If he did, he was in obvious danger of ridicule from his fellow-players and from members of the public who would retort, ' You tell us how to do it. But what a mess you make of it yourself ! ' There was never any suggestion that Shakespeare was an outstanding actor ; he only assisted with minor roles. He could fairly give lectures to dramatists, but as a tutor of acting he was on slippery ground.

But there are his accusations and we can understand why he made them. The acting of the time was essentially rhetorical. Oratory was part of the curriculum of a liberal education in ancient Greece and Rome ; and the men of the Renaissance, taking over the classical ideas and the classical discipline, both caught and relished fine, full speech. School plays were not performed for entertainment only : they were aids to the mastery of rhetoric. There was detailed instruction in gesture as well as in delivery, and this would be redoubled when a boy became apprenticed to the players.

If there was restlessness and rowdiness in the audience, it was necessary to project the voice lustily and to force attention by a style of acting which had a forthright attack and was garnished with picturesque poses. Here, naturally, lay temptation, and Shakespeare's criticisms of excessive strutting and bellowing and sawing of the air suggests that the temptation was often too much for the performers. In pictorial art Shakespeare was a realist, as we saw : he wanted the painting to be closely representative of the persons and the scene portrayed. In his counsel to the players, he shows that he was a realist also in the theatre and demanded an exact, subtle presentation of the dramatist's character in all his moods and movements.

That he had to fight for this is made plain by Hamlet's words, and the fight may often have been lost. Thus we can visualise Shakespeare groaning as he heard from the side of the stage or from behind the scenes his lines being thumped and banged across by a player who knew that by these methods he could get a round of applause from the groundlings and from the less judicious spectators among those in the galleries.

'And let those that play your clowns speak no more than is set down for them.'

Hamlet, having dealt with the exaggerated antics of the tragedians, went on to censure the 'antic' fellows themselves, the clown or clowns of his and other companies. When we use the word 'clown' we must distinguish between the circus clown and the comedian. The authentic clown is really a soloist and works in a world of his own ; it is a world of fantasy, not reality. He is not playing 'let's pretend' as actors are playing it ; he is not attempting to be anybody whom we can meet and recognise in day-to-day life. He is himself alone, a fool or zany, whose actions are incalculable and absurd. Especially he represents the unruly element in man. He defies authority ; he steals the sausages and chases the policeman with a red-hot poker. He is human nature uninhibited and by no means exemplary. His home is not a stage where human conduct is being represented ; it is the arena where fancy-free is the order, or rather the disorder, of the day.

A droll whose chief function is to take liberties can hardly fit easily or comfortably into a team of actors. If he is told to enact his part in a play, he will break loose and indulge in his own kind of hilarious nonsense. That is what the author of a play resents, while many of the public, or at least ' some quantity of barren spectators ', as Hamlet called the unruly clown's admirers, are roaring with laughter. As the Elizabethan drama developed, the clown was put under some discipline : his parts were brought into line with the reasonable performance of a play. He was instructed to be a comedian and conform to order—and he did not like it.

In order to give the clown some scope outside the play, the performances, even of the most serious plays, were often ended with what was called ' a jig '. This was a musical sketch with a little farcical story, music, dancing, and tomfoolery. When Platter was taken across the Thames to a Bankside theatre in 1599 he saw a play about Julius Caesar, presumably Shakespeare's, and after it dancers, two dressed as men and two as women. What struck him was the excellence of the dancing rather than the drollery ; but what he saw must have been one of the jigs, of which Shakespeare spoke with contempt. When Hamlet is disparaging Polonius's taste in theatrical matters, he says that the old man must be entertained with something indecent or else a jig : otherwise he will fall asleep. When in our own time we occasionally maintain the age-long ritual of the harlequinade, in which the clown is let loose as a law-breaker, we properly attach it to a pantomime and to the unreal world of fairy stories : Shakespeare, to his disgust, had to see a similar set of clownings and caperings occupy the stage after the most serious of his plays.

There was bound to be trouble, and Will Kempe, the chief clown in Shakespeare's company, the Lord Chamberlain's Men in the fifteen-nineties, parted from them. During the wars in the Netherlands (1585–6) he had been abroad with the Earl of Leicester as an entertainer to his lordship and the troops. He had been alluded to in 1590 as the successor to a famous clown called Tarleton ; Kempe, as jest-monger, was called heir to Tarleton's ghost. Later he took parts in Shakespeare's plays, being Peter in *Romeo and Juliet*, which is a trifle, and Dogberry in *Much Ado About Nothing*, which is quite a ' fat ' part, as actors say. He was one of the leaders of the ' fellowship ' and one of the original shareholders of the Globe. He may have been one of the dancers seen by Platter. But in 1599 he left them and achieved the spectacular feat, and one dear to a natural soloist and exhibitionist, of dancing his way from London to Norwich, making money as he went on this marathon of capering merriment and enjoying the sense of being his own master now, with no dramatist to curb him.

The clowns in the comedies were often cast as comic servants. They could be sly fellows, prototypes of the famous Jeeves of our time, or simple blunderers. In the tragedies there was naturally less scope for their larking ; they were given characters proper to the story and single scenes, such as that of the Grave-diggers in *Hamlet* and of the Porter at the castle-gate in *Macbeth*. They must have resented this limitation and doubtless insisted on a good chance to win laughter in the following jigs. Clown parts reappear with the roles of Trinculo and Stephano in *The Tempest*, but for a time they had been replaced by something subtler.

It is generally supposed that when Will Kempe left Shakespeare's company, his place was taken by Robert Armin, who was more of an actor and less of an ' antic ' : he was a lettered man, too, and wrote plays, though not with success. It is believed that he acted Touchstone in *As You Like It* ; that is a robust part which Kempe

147

might have heartily tackled. But Kempe would not have suited the gentler, even pathetic, roles of Feste in *Twelfth Night* and the Fool in *King Lear*. Here Armin's presence is supposed to have shaped the writing of the parts with their call for a lighter style and a more delicate singing voice. Both these are waif-like creatures in whom the compulsion to jest, under penalty of the whip, was a painful service and even a tragical fate. The droll with an aching heart is one of the theatre's oldest favourites. Shakespeare, with his sure theatrical instinct, understood that the pathos ' Laugh, clown, laugh ', when the clown would rather be staying glum and silent in a corner, was certain to move an audience.

So, with the development of fine shades of character-acting, the clown ceased to be the libertine, the anarchist, and the leader of a crazy gang when the theatre took over some portion of the long popular Feast of Fools. This revel was one of great antiquity, going right back to the Roman Saturnalia, when even the slaves were for a while allowed the privileges of their owners and had licence to be uproarious. The Christian Church turned this into the mediaeval Feast of Fools, at which servants briefly took the place of masters. There was much indulgence of the spirit of ' let's pretend ' ; men dressed as women and women as men ; there was also wearing of animal disguises. (This shows how ancient is our still surviving tradition of pantomime in which the ' principal boy ' is played by a girl, the ' dame ' by a man, and there is nearly always an animal, cat, horse, or cow, as the story demands, enacted by a human mimic or by two of them representing fore and hind legs.)

The clown as a figure outside the story, an independent droll in a world of his own, survives in the modern circus, where he still wears the ancient trappings, make-up, and marks of his calling. For centuries he has assumed the bald head with the single tuft of hair in the middle of it. He is the everlasting popper-up and Jack-in-the-box. He is also the everlasting tripper-up, the scamp and scallywag who sends law-and-order sprawling, not without some tumbles of his own. The clown is still ' he who gets slapped ' and must take what comes to him. We used to meet him to perfection in the early films of Charlie Chaplin, down-at-heel, down-and-out, but ever defiant, ever escaping. Norman Wisdom began as pure clown with his knock-me-down acrobatics. He went on to become an actor : in that he has been typical of the change that befell clowning in Shakespeare's lifetime. The lonely figure was absorbed in a co-operation of comedy.

We may surmise that Shakespeare, after his protests against the tragedian who would out-Herod Herod and the fool who would over-play his folly, did get what he wanted : tragical acting that was reasonably true to life instead of being unrestrainedly false to life, and performance of comedy which was also close to reality instead of being tumultuous tomfoolery with little or no regard for what Hamlet called the ' necessary question of the play '. In Ben Jonson's work the comedian, with recognisable imitation of actual characters, replaced the ' antic ' altogether. But you cannot keep Jack-in-the-box completely boxed. He made his way into the ring and the arena. On the stage in following centuries he found a niche in pantomime and its sequel, the harlequinade.

With limited possibilities of scenic effect, costume could be employed, when money sufficed, to bedeck the stage and do honour to a place or a period. Not that there was any attempt to offer accurate presentation of far-off countries and of king-doms long ago. We have plain proof that the players, confronted with a classical tale, laid hands on whatever was available to create their picture of antiquity. We have a contemporary drawing by Henry Peacham of a scene from *Titus Andronicus* in which Titus is attired as an ancient Roman ; the kneeling Queen might be drawing on a regal wardrobe of any epoch and the attending pikemen, capped and breeched, might be the guards of a monarch

Illustration by Henry Peachum for *Titus Andronicus*

in Shakespeare's own time. Aaron the Moor is made up to look as black as his own character in the play and shows plenty of ebony skin at either end of his tunic.

The Renaissance artists of Italy were apt to depict classical heroes in this kind of assorted haberdashery. A medieval doublet could accompany a Roman helmet with metal greaves to act as shin-pads for the warrior's naked legs. Paulo Veronese was a painter who handsomely indulged a fancy both classical and romantic by assembling the foppery as well as the battle-dress of all the ages, mixing plumage and metal plate. That is a fashion which has returned to the stage in our time. Sixty years ago it was the custom to produce Shakespeare with complete antiquarian accuracy. The armour and heraldic insignia of a historical play had to be correct in detail, and learned specialists were employed to see that it was so. The great productions directed by Beerbohm Tree were scrupulous, as well as lavish, in reproducing the costumes of ancient Rome, or of the Middle Ages. But now the stage-decorator and costumier has reverted to older practice. We put Tudor plays into Jacobean dress, or even contemporary dress, as the great actors of the eighteenth century did before us, playing their Macbeths and Romeos in the silks and wigs of a Georgian beau. Or we accept the Veronese example (and also that revealed in the drawing of *Titus Andronicus*) and make the best not only of both worlds, but of many.

It is shown in the accounts of the manager Henslowe that he was prepared to pay out handsomely for costumes, a course which he did not favour when it came to dealing with his penurious authors. Bridges-Adams, considering Henslowe's accounts, says that some of his expenditure would seem ' hair-raising ' to a producer of our time. ' Twenty pounds or so for a cloak is two hundred or more in the money of today. The lavish Irving did not use cloth of gold, finding that under gaslight much cheaper stuff looked better : in the more searching light of day Henslowe did and it cost him the equivalent of five pounds a yard. Sixteen shillings (say eight pounds) for copper lace or silver to lace a pair of hose is another entry.' We know that Alleyn played Marlowe's *Tamburlaine* in a splendour of copper lace.

For costumes of their own period the players had various sources of supply. There was the second-hand shop where a dandy out of funds might pawn his finery. Some clothes for stage use were got from the valets of the great, as Platter chanced to discover. Commenting on the expensive and elaborate costumes to be seen on the London stage he said that it was the English custom for the lords and knights to bequeath even the best of their wardrobe to their serving-men. The recipients found it embarrassing to be seen abroad in such costly glory : it might give a wrong impression of what they had in their purses. So they sold their fine suits ' for a little money ' to the actors. Probably they were able to drive a better bargain than

Platter suggests. In any case, here was, for the players, a reasonably economical source of elegance. They would take the eye of the audience and persuade the spectators that they were indeed looking on true men of wealth and fashion and not on ill-clad mummers vainly pretending to be princes and plutocrats.

Music in the Tudor theatre was plentiful. The trumpets proclaimed the opening of the play ; the historical dramas resounded with the drums. The strings heightened the emotion of a tragic scene. The song and dance of the jig sent the spectators away with a laugh and a melody. In between, there had been incidental music and the songs written into the plays by the dramatist. The acting company were expected, as indeed was everybody in that period, to have an ear for music and some skill in singing or performance. But there were also regular musicians attached to a team. When the Capulets are giving their ball in *Romeo and Juliet* we read ' Enter musicians ' and the musicians are expecting further work (and are deprived of it) when Juliet fails to appear for her marriage to Paris. With them is one alluded to as ' the singer '. So, with the instrumentalists there was a special vocalist. To what extent the musicians were also small-part actors is uncertain.

The singer might accompany himself on the lute, or have the aid of a skilled lutanist. Soft music, for emotional scenes, was supplied by ' a consort of viols '. Music was particularly linked with unnatural and supernatural events. ' Strange and solemn ' music accompanies Prospero's magic in *The Tempest*. When people seemingly dead are restored to life, as in the case of Hermione in *The Winter's Tale* and Thaisa in *Pericles*, music is demanded. Cerimon, the doctor who revives Thaisa after her immersion in a sea-flung coffin, is precise about this. ' The viol once more,' he commands as he goes about his curative business. There was weird music in *Macbeth* for the weird sisters, or witches, before the roll of drums announced the Thane and his troop.

The range of implements was large. The hautboy, a wooden double-reed instrument, was in frequent use. So was the rebeck, a stringed instrument. The cithern was a guitar played with a plectrum or quill. It was frequently kept in barbers' shops for the use of the waiting customers. Three of the musicians in *Romeo and Juliet* are named Rebeck, Catling, and Soundpost. Catling was the catgut which made a rebeck's strings, and a soundpost was the supporting peg in the framework of a rebeck or violin.

The clown was often a melody-maker. Of Tarleton we have a woodcut, showing him with pipe and tabor or drum. Will Kempe, dancing to Norwich, could hardly have had the extra energy to be his own musician. We have a picture of him with a companion who has the pipe and drum. That the actors themselves were musical performers was shown in the will of Shakespeare's colleague, Augustine Phillips, who left to his late apprentice Samuel Gisborne his bass viol or 'cello and to the succeeding apprentice James Sands his cithern, bandore, and lute. The amount of music in the plays grew when there was the move to indoor theatres and to increasing inclusion of the masque. The musicians had their special room in the theatre, probably in the gallery above the inner stage when that was not being used for some action of the play. They could be moved here and there about the stage, as we have seen, in *Romeo and Juliet* or under it as occurred in *Antony and Cleopatra*. In that play the musicians had to supply dance-tunes for the revel on Pompey's galley and then the sound of hautboys under the stage to provide some ominous strains signifying disaster for Antony. ' Music i' the air,' says one soldier. ' Under the earth,' says another. The performers in that play, laying on ' flourishes ' to welcome the great ones and ' alarums ' for battle-music, as well as attending revels and providing ghostly admonitions, were in full employment.

153

Shakespeare's own knowledge and appreciation of music is obvious from the many allusions in his plays. Harmony to him, and to the Elizabethan mind, was one of the principles of a good life in politics as well as in the arts. He loathed a discord in affairs

Will Kempe dancing to Norwich

' To jig off a tune at the tongue's end, canary
to it with your feet, humour it with turning
up your eyelids. . . .'

Love's Labour's Lost

of state as much as he loathed a jarring note upon his ear. Harmony was proportion, and harmony was order, with all degrees agreeing. Ulysses, in *Troilus and Cressida*, laying down the rules of politic life, exclaims,

Take but degree away, untune that string,
And hark what discord follows ! Each thing meets
In mere oppugnancy.

154

The stars in the sky maintain their order. The cosmos is like music, a composition. In an often-quoted speech in *The Merchant of Venice* Lorenzo moralises upon the discipline of 'Sweet consort' in all sections of the universe.

> How sweet the moonlight sleeps upon this bank !
> Here will we sit, and let the sounds of music
> Creep in our ears : soft stillness and the night
> Becomes the touches of sweet harmony.
> Sit, Jessica. Look, how the floor of heaven
> Is thick inlaid with patines of bright gold :
> There's not the smallest orb which thou behold'st
> But in his motion like an angel sings,
> Still quiring to the young-eyed cherubins ;
> Such harmony is in immortal souls ;
> But whilst this muddy vesture of decay
> Doth grossly close it in, we cannot hear it.

So the musicians entered at Portia's Belmont. So, too, they entered to grace all his comedies, especially *A Midsummer Night's Dream* and *Twelfth Night*. Continually the play is indebted to their presence. That they must have been adept and reliable in this art is implicit in the poet's praise of music. Lorenzo could not be let down. Suppose that after so high a praise of harmony the little orchestra had only responded by

> Straining harsh discords and unpleasing sharps

one can imagine the dramatist being very rude in his comment and possibly drastic in his action. For Shakespeare by this time had managerial rank : he had a reputation for gentleness, but one cannot think that he would have easily pardoned any musician who made mockery of his repeated praise of 'heavenly harmony'.

A subject on which more information would be valuable is the amount of preparation given to a play in Shakespeare's time. Scholars have had enough of the raw material of information wherewith to build the most complicated arguments over the structure of the Elizabethan theatre, which, in any case, could have been in a few days altered to suit new needs by an enterprising manager with a few masons and carpenters. There has, on the other hand, been very little discussion of the really more important question, how and by whom the rehearsals were directed. The reason for that is partly lack of evidence and partly the ignorance of some scholars (not all) about working conditions in the theatre. Some of them appear to imagine that if the dramatist supplies a good text and the manager provides a team of players and a theatre of some sort, the job is done and a good play, even a masterpiece, will surely result.

But the masterpiece in the theatre is the product of intricate co-operation and of clever production which will employ that co-operation fruitfully. In the theatre of today we have a pro-ducer, as he or she has been called, or director, a name used in America and increasingly used in Britain. The producer is partly responsible for casting the play and wholly responsible for welding together the effects of acting, scenery, lighting, costume, and so on : there are separate artists and technicians working with him in the provision of these decorations and enhancements. But there must be one controller. It is true that the Elizabethan theatre was much simpler than our own, but it had its music, its painted cloths, its ' noises off ', its stage-fights in plenty, and its wardrobe. Who took charge ?

In the simple rustic mummery presented in *A Midsummer Night's Dream*, Quince the Joiner has that office of command which he exercises very gently. He has ' the scroll ' with the players' names and is asked to make a roll-call. Then he is to tell the actors ' what the play treats on and so grow to a point '. The company ' spreads itself ' and are told which parts they will play ; when these have been allotted and explained, they are to meet again and rehearse.

Quince after that acts, in a very mild way, as producer and prompter. And this procedure of the Athenian amateurs was probably an elementary version of what happened in Shakespeare's professional theatre. But unfortunately we have few facts on which to estimate the length and nature of the rehearsals and the methods of their conduct. The vocabulary of the theatre has changed little since Tudor times. They used the terms ' rehearsal ', ' prompter ', ' wardrobe ', and ' the book ', the last signifying the text of the play. But we do not hear of a producer. The nearest we come to this is in the mention of a ' guider '. In the passage quoted from Dekker about the troublesome bucks who took sixpenny seats on the stage, it was stated that a fellow of this kind would ' presume to be a guider and stand at the helm to steer the passage of scenes '. This describes the office of the producer ; but whether guider was the regular name for such a person or simply an invention of Dekker's we cannot tell.

Who then guided a Shakespearian production ? Was it the dramatist or the leading actor. Shakespeare himself or Burbage ? Shakespeare, as author, knew what he wanted, and as one who had spent his life in the theatre, acting, writing, and managing, he would also, at least after his apprenticeship, have known how to get it. As a small-part actor he had the chance to slip across from the stage to the auditorium when his lines had been spoken. If it is true that he played Old Adam in *As You Like It* and the Ghost in *Hamlet*, he could have combined his performance with the larger labours of production. Burbage, on the other hand, with enormously long parts to tackle, was needed on the stage nearly all the time at rehearsals. It is true that actor-managers in our time have been able to combine the functions of protagonist and producer ; but it is not a practice generally advocated or likely to produce the best results.

So we may hazard a guess that Shakespeare directed his own

rehearsals : there is evidence that Ben Jonson did so in the case of his plays, but Jonson was not continuing to be an actor, as Shakespeare was. One of the fascinating problems of Shakespeare's life is his use of his time. If he were directing rehearsals all morning, acting in the afternoon and also at night, if the company were called to the Court or to one of the Inns of Court or a nobleman's house, how did he find leisure to write plays at the rate of two major pieces every year ? I am surprised that the anti-Shakespearians, eager to prove that Shagsper the actor cannot have been Shakespeare the author, never seized on this point. Furthermore, if Shakespeare went out on tour with his company, the difficulty of concentration upon authorship, while jogging along on horseback from town to town, would have been more acute.

One must assume that Shakespeare was good at sitting up half the night. The frequent allusions in his plays to the horrors of sleeplessness and the blessing of sleep have caused people to think that he suffered from insomnia. In that case, he would often prefer the desk to the bed. There is a passage in Ben Jonson's *Discoveries* which describes a man who ' when he hath set himself to writing, would join night to day, press upon himself without release, not minding it till he fainted . . . he would work out of himself what he desired, but with such excess as his study could not be ruled. . . .' This Dover Wilson thinks ' probably referred to Shakespeare ', and I agree about the probability. It explains how Shakespeare could both compose, act in, and produce his plays ; it also explains why he seems to have been exhausted and eager to spend much more time in Stratford well before he was fifty.

Of course Burbage may have collaborated with him closely : actors and authors quarrel easily, but there is no report of dissensions in Shakespeare's ' fellowship of players '. The fact that they remained as colleagues for twenty years is strong evidence of compatible temperaments. Nowadays we have specialists to

Richard Burbage

'The deep tragedian . . .
    ghastly looks
Are at my service, like
    enforced smiles,
And both are ready in
    their offices'

Richard III

supervise certain parts of a production. You may see on your programme 'Fights arranged by so-and-so'. One of Shakespeare's company may have been in charge of the numerous duels and battles that occur in the plays ; if so, the allusion to 'ragged foils' and 'brawl ridiculous' was unkind and probably, in the event, omitted. Since the jigs were disliked by Shakespeare, the direction of these would have been left to the First Clown, who could thus compensate himself if his antics in the play itself had been disliked and cut down by the author-producer.

I can find no evidence about the length of Elizabethan rehearsals. They can hardly have had the time and attention devoted to them in our time. At Stratford-upon-Avon, about six weeks are now given to each production, and this is made possible by limiting the programme to five plays in each year, and spacing out these presentations between March and August. But the work can be done very

much faster and often very well by producers less ' perfectionist '.
At Stratford six plays used to be hurried on, and often with excellent
results, in rapid succession at the start of the season. This meant no
more than ten rehearsals to each play and these spaced out over many
weeks. Probably this was as much as Shakespeare himself ever had.

Dr Leslie Hotson in *The First Night of Twelfth Night* has suggested that this exquisite piece was written, rehearsed and presented
within a fortnight. This seems to me incredible. That the piece
could have been staged in that time for production before the Queen
at Whitehall, which would mean a polished and fully prepared
performance, is possible ; but that Shakespeare was scribbling away
during the fourteen days and handing the text in strips to his company
is beyond my belief. He may have altered some names and written
in some lines to a play already in being to suit the occasion when the
Italian grandee, Count Orsini, visited London and that he introduced,
for example, the play's lordly lover as Orsino is likely enough. It
is likely also that the actors could jump quickly to a new task, but
that both author and actors could jump together at the speed
mentioned by Dr Hotson is not at all probable. The tradition that
The Merry Wives of Windsor was written, under royal command, in
a fortnight is credible. The play is a rough one, mostly in prose,
and shamelessly exploits the same situation three times over, sug-
gesting that the author had no time to be inventive. There is no
tradition that it was also produced within the same brief space.

Whoever directed the productions of a play, the number of
rehearsals cannot have been great. No piece could enjoy a long
run, and new work was continually brought in because the audience
was so limited. During Shakespeare's working life London is supposed to have been a city of two hundred thousand people ; dis-
counting the children, the Puritans who hated the theatre on moral
grounds, the very poor, and those who enjoyed only bear-baitings
and public executions for their entertainment, we have a probable

potential audience of fifty thousand at the most. If a fifth of these visited a play it was a great success. Nashe, in a pamphlet called *Pierce Penniless* (1592) records the popularity of *Henry VI*, Part I in that year, and speaks of 'there having been ten thousand spectators at least'. But ten thousand would soon be used up. That is about the number that would attend a successful play in our time in ten days.

If, for example, the Haymarket Theatre in London were playing to its capacity of nine hundred seats, as this popular house often does, it would take more than eleven performances to hold that ten thousand; say, rather, twelve, allowing for matinées attracting less than capacity. The number that could be held in the Tudor theatres was probably similar, although they must have varied considerably according to the size of the building and the number of groundlings who could be squeezed into the standing-room in case of 'a sell-out'. We know that *Henry VI*, Part I, so much beloved for the figure of 'brave Talbot' and his heroic part in the French wars, had fourteen performances, which was deemed a triumph. Many other plays were able to last only two or three days.

The management did not, as a rule, stage plays for a run; a number of them were put into repertory, as we say, and acted in rotation according to demand. There is valuable evidence about these matters in the papers of Philip Henslowe, who was in management with Edward Alleyn, Burbage's rival in skill and popularity, as his leading player. In Henslowe's six seasons at the Rose Theatre between 1594 and 1597 there were performances given during one hundred and twenty-six weeks, in which time fifty-five new or newly revised plays were offered; that is nearly one a fortnight. At the same time the favourites, especially the plays of Marlowe, were kept constantly on the programme. Shakespeare and his fellows worked under similar conditions and had to keep finding new pieces and injecting them into the repertorial stream. During most of his time Shakespeare was himself responsible for contributing a new one every six months.

It is therefore a fair surmise that no new play was given what we would deem adequate preparation, judged by the London standards of today. The fortnight of its rehearsals was not a clear one, since performance of other plays were going on every afternoon and possibly in private premises at night. Into this hustle there had to be combined the learning of the parts (some enormously long), the guiding of the action, the scheming of fights, the schooling of the apprentice players, and the arrangement of the music, costumes armour, weapons, and of such simple scene-cloths as were used. Dress rehearsals, with all ' effects ' ready, had to be fitted in. The production had to be quickly ready : it may have been, one can almost conclude must have been, unready sometimes and always fairly rough.

The acting companies were not large in size : expenses had to be kept down. So doubling and trebling of the minor roles were carefully practised. Platter said that he saw *Julius Caesar* acted by ' some fifteen people '. The cast list of the play in modern editions contains thirty-four characters apart from citizens and soldiers. We are used to impressive crowds in the Forum and sizeable armies in the subsequent fighting. But Shakespeare's audience was ready to see a crowd when it heard a clamour and to imagine a regiment when it heard the roll of a drum.

Rehearsals were carried on under discipline. Late-comers and absentees were fined, and that heavily. Unpunctuality at rehearsal cost a whole day's pay ; not to be properly costumed and ready at hand at the right minute on the day of performance cost three times as much. The under-rehearsed actor had the help of a big sheet called the Plot posted up somewhere behind the stage. Here were listed entrances and cues and, if a man were playing two or three minor roles without much preparation and in the midst of a repertory of other plays, he would need this information about the story of the present piece and about his various contributions to it.

Nowadays plays are given plenty of publicity by advertising, by sending out news paragraphs and photographs, by stimulating discussion ' on the air ', or by showing excerpts on television screens. All we know of Tudor publicity is that bills were posted about the town announcing the play and outlining its particular attractions. It was hoped that this would make a sufficient section of the public ready for the moment when the flag was run up on the theatre's tower and the trumpets sounded, while nervous men and boys behind the stage were having a last glance at the Plot or at the strips of paper with their ' lines '.

CHAPTER EIGHT

Actors and Authors

THE actors were organised in companies which carried the name of their patrons. These patrons were not so much financial backers as social assets and guarantors of respectability. An Act of 1572, passed that is to say when Shakespeare was eight years old, classed as ' rogues and vagabonds ' all ' common players in interludes ' as well as minstrels and bear-wardens unless they belonged to the Crown itself or to a man of title or high degree. To say that they ' belonged ' did not imply more than working under a vague supervision. Lord So-and-So's Men, as the team would be called, went their own ways, chose their own plays, and faced their own risks, and, if they got into financial difficulties through failure of their plays or the incidence of plague, the nobleman did not necessarily keep them on his personal pay-roll. To have players carrying his name might be a cause of pride, as well as of entertainment. If they were a cause of trouble, he could drop them.

The players themselves had to make their own arrangements for buying their wardrobe and properties as well as their plays and for leasing or building a London theatre. They did this by pooling what money they had or could raise, each holding shares according to their contribution of funds. The sharers usually included the leading actors ; they were the important people : under them there were the ' hired men ' and the boy apprentices who were taken on by the sharers and taught their business. These boys frequently had very large and important parts, but their status was lowly and their rewards lay chiefly in the training they received which would give them a profitable future, if they showed energy and talent. Their lives were strenuous and the discipline severe.

We are so much accustomed to women players who may be the most magnetic ' stars ', with names and faces widely known, that it is strange to find that the Tudor boy actors, on whom so much depended, were treated as insignificant youngsters, except in the companies limited to children. One would have thought that the town would have been ringing with the name of the boy who played Shakespeare's Juliet, since the play of *Romeo and Juliet* was a great success and much talked about. But we hear nothing of him and we do not know who played the part. Ben Jonson wrote a poem on the death of a child called Salathiel Pavy who died at the age of eleven and was renowned for taking old men's parts in a children's company ; and later on there was a boy called Dicky Robinson who did become a well-known figure. He is mentioned in the list of the King's Men included in the First Folio of Shakespeare's plays printed in 1623, and the town relished his mimicry of women.

One of the sharers would act as business manager. Heminge, one of the editors of the First Folio, held that office in Shakespeare's ' fellowship '. That he received the payments for Court performances indicates his position. Among the hired men, whose natural ambition was to rise to be sharers, were the wardens of the costumes and the keepers of the books of the plays : the latter were responsible for having the texts available and for prompting at performances. The companies either rented theatres in London from a man of capital such as Henslowe and Langley, who owned respectively the Swan and the Rose, or set up for themselves as theatre purchasers or theatre builders. Shakespeare was one of those who built and shared in the open Globe Theatre and took over, nearly ten years later, the covered house in Blackfriars.

The money paid for seats or standing-room by the public was divided up in various ways. If the theatre belonged to a landlord and not to the actors playing in it, there was an agreement that he took the receipts from one section of the theatre while the players took the rest. If the players owned their own theatre, then the proceeds were divided between the two different kinds of sharers : some sharers had an interest in the theatre buildings and drew their dividends on the profits of this ownership as well as receiving their portion due to them as actor-sharers. It was possible for a thrifty man to do very well for himself if his company were successful. That Shakespeare himself was thrifty as well as successful is shown by his considerable investments in land and property in Stratford as well as in London. The theatre owners or theatre sharers had to provide, keep up, and equip the building ; the actor-sharers selected the plays and hired and fixed the apprenticeships. They also arranged for purchase and maintenance of the costumes and obtained the necessary permission to perform the dramas they had chosen.

Licences to perform were obtained from a Court official, the Master of the Revels. There is much grumbling about the Stage Censorship which exists in Britain today. The Elizabethans worked under a discipline of their own. The high authorities liked to have players about to entertain them ; they did not want them to criticise policy or express unusual opinions. Plays with religious or political topics were closely supervised and might be forbidden altogether. Profanity was ruled out, and in the reign of King James the standards of propriety in language were tightened. We know that oaths involving God's name were dropped from the text of Shakespeare's plays when the new rules came in. In 1597 a play called *The Isle of Dogs* by Nashe ran into serious trouble on a charge of being seditious and slanderous. The performers of it, Lord Pembroke's Men, were committed to prison ; Ben Jonson, who may have had a hand in the piece, was sent with others to the Marshalsea gaol. The author escaped to the country. Jonson was accustomed to the cells. He was in prison four times, three of them for injudicious writing.

Another play to come under censorship was a chronicle about the life of Sir Thomas More, in which Shakespeare probably took a hand and may have left us, in the manuscript which we possess, a specimen of his own handwriting. More was Lord Chancellor under Henry VIII and was executed for refusing to accept the Act of Supremacy whereby the King of England became head of the Church in England. So Sir Thomas, as one who had opposed the Protestant Reformation, was a dangerous subject in the eyes of the authorities. Moreover the play included scenes of rebellion, another kind of spectacle unpopular at Court. The Master of the Revels, then Sir Edmund Tilney, wrote on the manuscript ' Leave out the insurrection wholly.' It seems that in the end the players took fright ; the whole play was left out wholly and remained unacted.

There was another example of the Court resentment against injudicious topics when the members of Shakespeare's company were in trouble for giving a specially commissioned performance of *Richard II* on the eve of the Essex Rebellion in 1601. The play showed the deposition of a monarch : that, when a revolt against the Crown was being planned, was obviously a theme that the Queen would find objectionable, especially when acted by the Lord Chamberlain's Men, who were virtually her own servants. Fortunately they escaped with a warning, probably because they had a good record and friends at Court.

The actors who rose to be sharers did well for themselves and had houses in the country, either far out as Shakespeare did at Stratford, or in the near-to-London pleasaunces. Alleyn of the Admiral's Men owned the Manor of Dulwich and was founder of Dulwich College. Of the King's Men Augustine Phillips had a place by the river at Mortlake; Henry Condell lived out at Fulham. Lowin, creator of Falstaff, retired to keep an inn at Brentford and is said to have died poor. But while the actors with a high position in their craft were able to save and invest, others were spendthrifts, and Henslowe admitted that he could only keep a hold on some of his players by keeping them in his debt. But, compared with the players, it was the authors who had a hard time. There were too many of them ready to knock out a piece, and the competition kept their earnings very low. Henslowe would pay twenty pounds for a sufficiently imposing stage costume, but he got his plays for an average price of six pounds: that was not 'in advance of royalties', i.e., in advance of percentage payments for each performance, but a fee which conveyed the play to the purchaser for his use when, where, and as often as he wished.

There was no law of copyright and the authors had no rights in what they wrote. The company owned the texts and tried to keep them from publication, lest others steal them for their own performances. A printer would pay two pounds for a pamphlet; a manager, like Henslowe, or a company, like Shakespeare's, paid six pounds for the text of a play and that was the end of the transaction. We do not know whether Shakespeare himself, when his success was established, drew special fees; but, whether he had his own rates for writing or not, he could never have become a man of property on his earnings with the pen. Nor can he have made much money as an actor, for his parts were small ones. It was chiefly as a sharer that he made the money which he kept and put into the purchase of land and houses.

His narrative poems, written early in his career, were issued with dedications to the Earl of Southampton, and it is likely that the Earl helped his protegé financially: the statement that Southampton gave

Shakespeare the sum of a thousand pounds was only made in 1709, long after Shakespeare's lifetime, by the editor of the plays, Rowe, who said that he had it from Sir William D'Avenant. The sum seems impossibly large : if a play could only fetch six pounds or so, this would be the equivalent of the rewards for one hundred and sixty-six plays—and Shakespeare in all his lifetime wrote thirty-six, probably collaborating in a few others. But these anecdotes usually had some foundation and Southampton may have treated Shakespeare handsomely. In any case, to have had the freedom of Southampton's house and company and to have associated with the Earl's Anglo-Italian secretary Florio, a dictionary-maker and translator of Montaigne's Essays, was a precious privilege. It has been made a matter of surprise that a young man from the country could so soon have been able to write about the nobility and their ways : the patronage extended by Southampton is the answer to that.

Ben Jonson said that in his whole life he never made more than two hundred pounds by writing plays. (Providing texts for Masques may have paid him better.) In his later life he received a royal pension as Poet Laureate, and the Earl of Pembroke allowed him twenty pounds a year for the purchase of books. But others were not so lucky. They scrambled for employment, which was sometimes given out in shares, each man to provide one section of the play and getting as little as one pound for his portion. The method of composition was for the author or authors to meet the manager or players, discuss a subject, rough out a plot, arrange parts to suit the talents of the actors, and then scribble away. For scribbling it was ; many plays were turned out hurriedly. The writers had the knack of 'bombasting out a blank verse' and could turn on the tap under pressure of their own hunger and thirst. We must not think of the Elizabethan stage as being everywhere littered with splendid writing because Shakespeare was one of its authors : it was, in fact, cluttered with hackwork. Most of the plays, as was

169

seen, had very short lives and had to be continually replaced. The writers had to accept the terms offered and turn out their bread-and-butter tragedies. They scribbled, they grumbled, and they consoled themselves in the taverns.

Robert Greene was a typical figure of the time. Born in 1558 he was schooled at Norwich, went to Cambridge, and then lived by his pen in London; he was known for his speedy writing of plays, pamphlets, and stories: he was dissolute and often in debt and did not live to see thirty-five. His colleague and rival Nashe was equally often dodging his creditors and was said never to have paid for his clothes or shoes. Greene's landlady so far forgave him for his unpaid rent that she put a laurel wreath on his dead body. That world—we meet it with Shakespeare's inn-hostess Mistress Quickly and the baggage Doll Tearsheet—had its squalor warmed, if not cleaned, with kindliness. The writers quarrelled and cursed and drank and made it up; they shared a common grievance, that against the actors who not only made more money than they did but acted as 'black-legs' in addition, breaking into the writers' market. It was urged by Greene against Shakespeare in his youth that he supposed himself a poet, being 'an absolute *Johannes Fac Totum*' (i.e., Jack-of-all-trades, author as well as actor) and 'in his own conceit the only Shake-Scene in the country'.

The theatre folk had their special taverns. The Mermaid in Cheapside has been made famous for the wit and sparkle of its sessions by some often-quoted verses of Francis Beaumont. One of the drinking company was Thomas Heywood, who managed to live longer than most of his kind, dying at seventy-one. He was a master-scribbler and an example of the general pace of output, since he claimed to have written (or had a hand in) no less than two hundred and twenty plays. He left a tribute in verse to the nature of the tavern gatherings in which friendly familiarity was stronger than the jealousies and disputes:

Marlowe, renowned for his rare art and wit,
Could ne'er attain beyond the name of Kit . . .
Excellent Beaumont, in the foremost rank
Of the rarest wits, was never more than Frank.
Mellifluous Shakespeare, whose enchanting quill
Commanded mirth or passion, was but Will ;
And famous Jonson, though his learned pen
Be dipped in Castaly, is still but Ben.
Fletcher and Webster, of that learned pack
None of the mean'st—yet neither was but Jack.

Thomas Fuller, who wrote a book on those whom he deemed worthy to be called Worthies about half a century after Shakespeare's death, described the kind of argument that went on over the cups. ' Many were the wit-combats betwixt him [Shakespeare] and Ben Jonson.' He likened Jonson to a great, Spanish galleon and Shakespeare to the lighter English man-of-war. Jonson was ' far higher in learning, but solid and slow in his performances while Shakespeare, lesser in bulk but light in sailing, could turn with all tides, tack about, and take advantage of all winds by the quickness of his wit and invention.'

The greatest writers for the theatre during Shakespeare's lifetime were Christopher Marlowe, who fired his fancy and his ambition, and Ben Jonson, with whom he often argued a point and sometimes collaborated as a player. (He was one of the actors in Jonson's first comedy, *Every Man in His Humour*.) In 1587, when Shakespeare may already have settled in London and was just working his way into the service of the theatre, the town was ringing with the music of a new voice and acclaiming its vociferous and flamboyant owner. Ben Jonson was still acquiring his classical learning under William Camden at Westminster School, but Marlowe had arrived. His life story is worth the telling since in it there is so much that reveals the flash and temper of the time.

171

Born in February 1564, two months earlier than Shakespeare, this son of a Kentish shoemaker kindled one of the earliest and most fiery torches that ever lit up the pageant of our English poetry and play-writing. His own flame was snuffed out while he was in the blaze of youth. Would he have rivalled Shakespeare had their lives run parallel? Would Shakespeare have done so well without Marlowe's example and stimulation? These are fascinating questions. Before an effort is made to answer them, it is helpful to have the few certain facts of Marlowe's brief and brilliant career.

In 1579, at the age of fifteen, he went with a scholarship to the King's School, Canterbury, already an ancient and famous academy. While a boy in his home-town he had a grander background than had Shakespeare at Stratford-upon-Avon. He had plenty to see. The famous cathedral soared in splendour above him ; life surged in its Tudor fierceness about him. Canterbury, being on the main road from London to the Channel ports, swarmed with soldiers, sailors, and adventurers. Rough justice for rough men was common. There were six public executions in the city during Kit's boyhood. There was, for contrast, the pomp of Queen Elizabeth's Progress, when she stayed with Archbishop Parker in 1573. Pageantry and play-acting were frequent. It was a good school for a man of the theatre.

Another scholarship took young Marlowe to Corpus Christi College in Cambridge in 1581. Several writers-to-be, Greene, Nashe, and Gabriel Harvey, were undergraduates in Marlowe's time. The title of University Wits was being briskly earned. Marlowe stayed at Cambridge for some six years and at the end was refused an M.A. degree. But no less a power than the Privy Council of England wrote to say that he had done Her Majesty good service and deserved to be rewarded for his faithful dealings. So he got his M.A. But what was the service for which the Privy Council had so highly praised a youngster of twenty-three ?

During the fifteen-eighties the Government's Secret Service was largely increased by the crafty Sir Francis Walsingham, who recruited likely young men to act as special agents and carriers of confidential despatches. Just after Marlowe left Cambridge there were two names mentioned in Lord Burghley's list of such employees. They were Morley and Marlin—probably both identical with our Christopher Marlowe. Spelling of names was very vague at that time—there were at least seven different spellings of Shakespeare's name. Marlowe had been entered as Marlin at Cambridge.

But these jobs were intermittent. The young man had a second career in mind. He had found time to begin writing at Cambridge. In his college library lay the raw materials for a lurid historical drama on the upstart Middle Eastern conqueror, Tamburlaine. The play was at once accepted by the famous Edward Alleyn, who saw in it a great part for himself and a likely triumph for the Admiral's Men.

Marlowe's success was immediate and immense. Here was a new voice indeed, far more ambitious in grandeur of language and of metaphor than anything heard in the English theatre before.

> His raptures were
> All air and fire.

wrote Michael Drayton—and rightly. Shakespeare's arrival in London was lit by that conflagration.

The flame was kept aglow in a second Tamburlaine play, and after that in five more tragedies of which *Dr Faustus* proved the most famous. This powerful study of a soul risking damnation for the sake of the body's bliss was weak in its would-be humorous episodes, but magnificent in its praise of the pleasures of the world and superb in the doomed man's farewell to these delights.

Going up to London, Marlowe lodged near the northern theatres of the town. His life was violent, as we have already seen : he knew the prison cells and had been bound over to keep the peace. He was suspected of atheism and of holding ' monstrous opinions '. In 1593, at the age of only twenty-nine, he was killed in a violent quarrel.

He had gone to the Thames-side harbour of Deptford and visited the home (or tavern) of a widow called Mrs Bull ; he met company, walked in the garden, and supped. It was a long conference, possibly about Secret Service matters. It was probably also a thirsty one. His associates were tough characters. There was a dispute over the bill and Marlowe was fatally stabbed over the right eye.

So, in this mess of blood and squalid argument, passed ' the gentle shepherd ', as Shakespeare rather oddly called him, for there was little of pastoral tranquillity in his life. The theatre lost its leading writer of the time—for Shakespeare's fame was only just arising. As Marlowe had himself written, ' Cut is the branch that might have grown full straight '. It was not so much cut, in fact, as viciously hacked.

Now we can return to the original question. Would Marlowe, had he lived, have been the equal of Shakespeare ? It is hard to believe that. It is significant that he began with his best. The two Tamburlaine plays contain grand poetry but they are a vast, untidy panorama of tyrannical ambition and villainy. Next, in *Dr Faustus*, he rose to his highest use of imagination and of words to match his soaring fancy. But instead of improving after this, his later work shows a decline.

In his tragedy of *Edward II*, a weak king unfit for the crown and not desiring it, he had a subject similar to that of Shakespeare's *Richard II*. But Marlowe, good though his play is in parts, showed neither the psychological subtlety nor the exquisite handling of language that are to be found in Shakespeare's play. Another case for comparison, fatal to Marlowe, lies in *The Jew of Malta*. This is largely a crude melodrama and cannot be matched with the broad sympathies exhibited in *The Merchant of Venice*.

Again, Marlowe showed no capacity for comedy, in which Shakespeare was extremely rich. To comprehend all the moods of man was Shakespeare's gift, not Marlowe's. There is no evidence that the latter could ever have created a Falstaff. If the childish clowning in *Dr Faustus* was introduced by another, perhaps by one of the actors of clown's parts, as has been suggested, that could only have occurred because Marlowe lacked the power to write comedy scenes for himself.

There remains the second query. Would Shakespeare have done as well if Marlowe had not preceded him? The answer must be that Shakespeare owed a great deal to Marlowe. The influence of his heart-stirring rhetoric on a budding writer must have been magical. In an early play like that vivid study of criminal violence and of a royal murderer, *Richard III*, the echoes of Marlowe's voice are so strong that some think Marlowe had a share in the writing of it.

Marlowe could pour out a torrent of eloquent verse, but he showed no signs of steady application in order to improve his knowledge of the theatre and the demands that it makes upon a writer. Shakespeare was obviously patient, industrious, and eager to learn his craft up to the point of perfection. Marlowe, if he had lived and made money, might have ended his life in debauch instead of losing it in a brawl. But Shakespeare, himself more deserving the description of 'gentle shepherd', stuck to his acting and his writing and to the making of an income.

Yet the debt was there. Marlowe wrote a haunting line: 'Infinite riches in a little room'. He took the English language, sent it soaring out of the little room of the theatre, and made it rich indeed. He had discovered the treasure which Shakespeare was so wonderfully to use and so vastly to enhance.

With the death of Marlowe, Shakespeare rose : his poems as well as his plays were acclaimed ; but by 1600 the figure of Ben Jonson began to assume a dominant position. Shakespeare had gone steadily forward, liked as a man and approved as a worker. But he was not the completely outstanding figure that he is to us. Furthermore he was not, as Ben Jonson became, a conspicuous character who would naturally preside at any social gathering of the writers and the wits.

Jonson had Scottish blood. His father was a Protestant clergyman, but he died before Ben was born in 1573. The mother then married a Londoner, who was a master bricklayer. The boy was able to take the conventional and classical curriculum under a famous scholar, William Camden, at Westminster School ; the family could not afford to send him to a university. But he remained proud of his classical training. Though he admired Shakespeare and wrote in sincere devotion the well-known tributary verses that appeared in the First Folio of Shakespeare's plays, he always felt himself to be his rival's academic superior and therefore a more substantial figure in the world of letters. He believed that dramatic work, indeed all forms of writing, should be conducted with an eye upon tradition and with proper observance of accepted rules. To him Shakespeare was an unruly poet, inspired, perhaps, and profuse, but ' wanting art ', by which he meant rather what we should call artifice.

Deprived of the chance to be a University Wit he was apprenticed to his stepfather's craft. He left the building trade, however, to be a soldier, fought in Flanders, killed his man (so he claimed), and came back to use his pen instead of his pike. With all his gifts he lacked ' the enchanting quill ' which Shakespeare handled, but he displayed the greatest vigour and versatility and could write a tender English lyric as well as a Roman tragedy.

Ben Jonson
' Was he not held a learned man ? '
Henry VIII

Jonson first served the shrewd Henslowe, who was always quick in discerning talent. He began as one of what we now call a script-writing team. But he was too large to be only a colleague and broke away to work independently of any one employer, and it was Shakespeare's own company, the Lord Chamberlain's Men, who gave him an early and important success. This was in 1598 with a comedy called *Every Man in His Humour*. There is a story, which cannot be proved but may well be true, that this play had been rejected by the company, but that Shakespeare, who liked it greatly on reading it, personally insisted on its performance.

Jonson's most notable work was done between 1606 and 1616. His comedies best known today, comedies both bitter and boisterous in their exposure of villainy, are *Volpone*, which is a picture of human greed, and *The Alchemist*, in which fools are mocked and robbed by an impudent impostor. It was Jonson's way to take one kind of human characteristic in isolation and reveal its failures, scandals, or absurdities. He transferred the idea of dominant

13

'humours' from the world of the doctors to that of the actors. He set out to satirise the people in his plays as representatives of one prevailing quality. This made for the broad portraiture of types, less subtle than Shakespeare's presentation of individuals, but useful in the pursuit of broadly comic effects. He scourged the victims of his wit with force and fury, but he lacked sympathy with fools and knaves, and it is just that kind of compassionate comprehension which has given Shakespeare's comedies so wide an appeal.

In 1616 Jonson did what Shakespeare left for others to do : he collected, edited, and published his own plays so far written. Then he gave up the theatre for a while and wrote scripts for masques. There was a famous architect, Inigo Jones, to decorate them and there was no sparing of expense in the staging. But the words were regarded as less important than the spectacle. So it was a waste of Jonson's time and, in his boisterous way, he quarrelled with Jones, growling that 'painting and carpentry are the soul of masque'. He, as an artist in words, went back to the theatre and wrote more comedies, but with less success than before.

Jonson wrote with great power. He had unchallengeable gifts and talents. Why then is he so little acted in our time ? Partly because Shakespeare is acted so much. (If Jonson is put into the programme at Stratford-upon-Avon, the visitors are annoyed because they say they have come all that way to see a play of Shakespeare's in his own town and do not want to be fobbed off with another man's work.) But there is another reason. Jonson's work was often more immediate and more local in its interests than was that of his rivals. It is excellent matter for the historian of the period, but that does not make a good play.

He rightly said that Shakespeare was not for an age but for all time. When he wrote that, he probably believed that he himself was for all time too. But the amount of topical allusion in some of his comedies and his delight in his gigantic vocabulary make difficulties for us. Another handicap is his erudition. He would pour out his learning where it was unnecessary. His Roman tragedy *Sejanus*, for example, shows far more historical knowledge and classical lore than Shakespeare ever had ; but it has far less dramatic urgency than Shakespeare's *Julius Caesar* or *Antony and Cleopatra*. Jonson believed that he knew all the regulations for writing good plays ; but his delight in the playwright's discipline and in the avoidance of factual errors destroyed the delight of audiences in most of his plays after his own lifetime.

Jonson is now remembered for those acid studies of deliberate knavery, *Volpone* and *The Alchemist*, and for the vivid panorama of London life in *Bartholomew Fair*, while Shakespeare is remembered for a far greater proportion of his whole output. One cannot read about the London of that time without feeling Jonson's presence, whereas Shakespeare seems to us elusive and withdrawn. But it was the elusive genius that posterity has placed upon the throne which Jonson believed to be his by right.

Among the work of others in the theatre, two tragedies by John Webster, *The Duchess of Malfi* and *The White Devil*, loom out with a sinister glow of sulphurous fire from the multitudinous plays of the early seventeenth century. We know almost nothing of Webster's life which ended in 1634. He may have begun as an actor : there was a man of that name touring in Germany with English comedians in 1594. His success as a writer was not in levity : he excelled in horrors of a nightmare kind. But he did not stage his Italianate stories of desperate sufferings and inhuman cruelty merely to give thrills to the groundlings : he poured the best of poetry into the worst of human behaviour. In the midst of their torments his heroines can speak with Shakespearean simplicity and pathos :

> My soul, like to a ship in a black storm,
> Is driven I know not whither.

179

Webster was a masterly contriver of emotional hurricanes in which the orphans of the storm defy their end with a calm beauty. Bodily extinction was not to be feared by a woman

> Knowing to meet such excellent company
> In the other world

and ready to face strangling by her brutal executioners with

> Come, violent death,
> Serve for mandragora[1] to make me sleep,
> Go tell my brothers, when I am laid out,
> They then may feed in quiet.

For such a woman the famous Websterian epitaph was fitting :

> Cover her face : mine eyes dazzle : she died young.

Jonson could never have written like Webster at his finest, and Webster at his finest could write a passage that Shakespeare could have envied. But he lacked Shakespeare's astonishing power to stay on the summits ; his splendours are few. Incidentally, there is an introductory note to *The White Devil* which indicates the risks of production on an unroofed stage when the weather was cold. Webster deplored the lack of a full and sympathetic house, and put the blame on the dull time of winter and a presentation in a theatre ' open and bleak '.

Shakespeare's immediate successor in the service of his own company was a partnership, that of Francis Beaumont and John Fletcher. They came of more elevated stock than did most of the theatre men. The collaboration did not last very long, for Beaumont, who was buried in Westminster Abbey, died at thirty-two. Fletcher, who lived to be forty-six, continued working with other men as well as composing by himself. Both had wit, facility,

---

[1] Of the narcotic plant, mandragora, Shakespeare also made music in *Othello*.

and a ready hand with a romantic tale or a brazen kind of comedy. They knew their public and served the changing taste of the audience who liked something lighter than the heavy tragedy to which Webster and some others were obstinately faithful.

That audience did not approach the play in the way that we do now. We ask, as we watch the progress of a play, whether the plot is plausible. Why this, why that, we mutter. The Elizabethans and Jacobeans cared nothing for plausibility. We are astonished for example at stories in which a lover cannot recognise his lady because she has put on boy's clothing. But to them, if a character announced that he or she was disguised, then it was accepted that they were unrecognisable by their closest friends. There were no complaints if the play contained events which seem to us incredible. The play-goers on the Bankside wanted to savour the thrill of great moments ; if the situation of the characters was of an intensely exciting or terrifying kind, or if the situation drew from the characters the ' mighty line ' of a Marlowe or the sharp drive at the heart that came with the most poignant poetry of Webster and Shakespeare, that sufficed. At their crudest the spectators relished the sight of a mutilated body and a stage piled with corpses ; at their best they were rapt by sublimity of speech as the tragic heroes went to their doom. They were abundantly served with both ; they could sup full with horrors and have the noblest use of language to make the music for the fearful feast.

The writers had their rivals in the showmen and there was fierce competition in their own territory, the Bankside of South London. For there was situated Paris Garden, which became a most popular resort of those who took pleasure in gory spectacles. While the authors were attracting the public with plays in which murder ran riot, they had, next door to them, entertainments no less sanguinary in the rings and arenas where bulls and bears were baited. The pleasure to be derived from watching animals gored is sometimes defended, as in the case of modern bull-fights, by the skill and daring of the human participants. In the case of the Elizabethans, the men engaged were not taking much risk. Animal was pitted against animal, as in cock-fighting, a sport which is still occasionally discovered to be existing in our own time.

It was not until 1642 that the Puritans closed the Bear Garden of Southwark. Macaulay's taunt that 'the Puritans hated bear-baiting, not because it gave pain to the bear but because it gave pleasure to the spectators' may have contained some truth. But at least the supposed 'kill-joys' were putting an end to an occupation which seems to us to be revolting. The men of that period were not queasy in these matters. If the crowds were delighted to watch public floggings and executions with the added horrors of mutilation of the corpse, they could well enjoy, without qualms, the sanguinary conflicts of mastiffs with bulls and bears; and it was not only the rabble who were enraptured patrons of the Garden. The Queen herself attended, and the courtiers naturally followed her journey across the river to the sessions there provided.

There was nothing scandalous in public opinion about the provision of these pleasures. Alleyn, the actor of high repute, joined with Henslowe the manager. Both were as ready to stage a carnival of blood as a tragedy of Marlowe's. They were the owners and managers of Paris Garden and, under James I, had a royal appointment to be Masters of the Games there presented. Shakespeare, with his sympathy for hunted animals, could hardly have relished this rivalry, and the allusions in the plays to the ferocities of the entertainment provided by Alleyn and his fellow-showmen were hardly an advertisement for these performances. The French, discussing the English character and habits in *Henry V*, speak of the mastiffs as brave but stupid. 'Foolish curs that run winking into the mouth of a Russian bear and have their heads crushed like rotten apples.' Several times the tragic hero is likened to a bear tied to a stake and forced to ' stand the course '. The bears that did stand the course, time and again, became favourites of the town : their names were familiar. Shakespeare mentions one called Sackerson, in *The Merry Wives of Windsor*. The young fop Slender talks thus with Anne Page,

Why do your dogs bark so ? Be there bears i' th' town ?

Anne Page

I think there are, sir ; I heard them talk'd of.

Slender

I love the sport well ; but I shall as soon quarrel at it as any man in England. You are afraid, if you see the bear loose, are you not ?

Anne Page

Ay, indeed sir.

Slender

That's meat and drink to me, now. I have seen Sackerson loose twenty times, and have taken him by the chain ; but, I warrant you, the women have so cried and shrieked at it, that it passed :—but women, indeed, cannot abide 'em ; they are very ill-favoured rough things.

There were other popular victims of the ring, bears known to their fanciers as Harry Hunks, Tom of Lincoln, and so on.

The bears were chained to a long post and then assaulted by mastiffs. They fought back under handicap : their teeth had been pared down. But they could still bite and had their claws. The dogs were hurled back and wounded, possibly killed. When a wounded bear was thought to have put up ' a good show ' he was released and succeeded by another whose task was to reduce more canine heads to the state of crushed apples. Much the same procedure was followed in the case of the bulls. They could toss instead of claw, and the attendants had an appliance for catching the dogs thus thrown before they crashed to the ground.

Risks were, it is true, sometimes taken by the human agents, but they were only children ! Small boys were engaged to chase a blinded bear and whip it into fury : they stood the danger of being mauled if they failed to dodge their blundering victim. This must seem to us the most repulsive of all the exhibitions staged at Paris Garden. It is some comfort to know from Master Slender that at least some of the women were not amused.

To such competition the drama was exposed. Many of the public, following the royal example, must have been equally responsive to a display of endurance by Sackerson and of tragic acting by Alleyn or Burbage. That the one entertainment did not destroy the other is shown by Henslowe's investment in both : he was not one to damage his own business by destructive rivals. What is so extraordinary to us is the combined appetites of the Elizabethans for bestiality and beauty. While they were listening to the silver speech of a Shakespearean lover at the Globe, they might hear the roars and howls of tortured animals in the neighbouring garden. While some were enraptured by the treble voice of a boy playing Juliet or Viola, others were adding to the ugly tumult of the bears' arena by applauding another victory for the bleeding Sackerson or Hunks.

CHAPTER NINE

The Darkening Scene

BECAUSE of the victories over Spain, which culminated in the defeat of an invasion of Ireland, because of the great bursts of poetry and the rich laughter of the comic stage, because of wealth on the social surface and wit upon the lips of the patrons and the writers patronised, we think of the last years of Elizabethan England as full of confidence and cheerfulness. But, under the glitter and the glory, there had been much misery of the many and apprehension among the few. The sorry failure of the Essex Rebellion in 1601 had been followed by the trial and execution of a most notable Elizabethan. When Essex died, Shakespeare's champion, Southampton had gone to the Tower. There was, for a while, much less mirth in Shakespeare's writing and much more inclination to investigate the evil that men do and the doom of the evil-doer. In that devotion to tragedy Shakespeare was to analyse the follies and disasters of jealousy in *Othello*, of over-weening ambition in *Macbeth*, and of vanity and cruelty in the persons of *King Lear* and his daughters. Comedy, whether written by Shakespeare or Jonson, became sour and even savage at the turn of the century. There was reason for the change of mood. The writers were reflecting a general reaction against the earlier exuberance.

During the end of the sixteenth century there had been a rising wave of discontent. There had been failures of harvest on the farms and loss of trade in the cities. The countryside had been in terror of the unemployed. These were not then registered persons who applied for their legal ration of relief: they were 'vagabonds' who had to be kept under discipline. A harsh new Poor Law did a little to assist necessity and more to punish those judged to be wantonly idle. A continual and accumulating grievance was the sale of monopolies. By an old prerogative the monarch could grant to private individuals the sole right to deal in various commodities. These monopolies, which obviously opened the way to extortionate prices, were a scandal which the Queen did nothing for a long time to abate. Her favourites, who enjoyed these 'patents', were thus rewarded at the public expense. Elizabeth, who knew how to temper obstinacy with prudence when a situation became desperate, had in the end to promise 'reformation'. It was badly needed.

In November of 1601 the Queen, now in the sixty-ninth year of her age and the forty-fourth of her sovereignty, received the greetings of her Parliament with memorable words :

'Though God hath raised me high, yet this I count the glory of my crown, that I have reigned with your loves. . . . It is not my desire to live or reign longer than my life and reign shall be for your good. And though you have had, and may have, many mightier and wiser princes sitting in this seat, yet you never had, nor shall have, any that will love you better.'

She could speak thus with sincerity and the deep affection was returned by her subjects. The monopolies were a scandal, but the other troubles of the time were not, people felt, of her making. She was still the heroine, but the last act of her drama was coming to its close. In the next year she began to fail physically : yet she would have her entertainment still. Early in February 1603 the Chamberlain's Men were summoned to the riverside palace of Richmond ; they must have played with sadness of heart. The clowns would know the irony of jesting now. Soon the Queen lay sinking. At the Court Sir Robert Cecil was making the last arrangements to bring in the new King. On 24 March Queen Elizabeth died. At once messengers went galloping from Richmond to Whitehall and from London to Scotland ; and with no delay there was another galloper from Scotland, the new King himself.

Fortunately there was no struggle over the succession. Mary Stuart's only son, James VI of Scotland, had to be accepted and he had made acceptance easy by his Protestantism. He soon showed that he was determined to end a wasteful war and make peace with Spain. But he could not be suspect as a nominee of the Pope. He was far from being physically attractive ; his head was over-large, his tongue slobbered out of his mouth, his legs were infirm, and his eyes protruding and goggling. He was a queer, twisted person who had never recovered wholly from the dangers and horrors of a grim childhood. He was constantly afraid of assassination and wore quilted clothes to defend him from a dagger's thrust. But he was no Puritan and, though he hated the smoking of tobacco, he was very far from disliking wordly pleasures : he was a brave rider and in the hunting field lay one of his chief delights. The players soon knew that they had no need to be afraid of their future. The King had kept his own company of actors in Scotland and he at once promoted the Chamberlain's Men to be the King's Men in his new capital. He had made all haste with the long ride to England, and he made all haste upon arrival to show his zest for the theatre. The frowning Puritans of the City found themselves immediately snubbed by the new encouragement of the players.

Only ten days after his arrival in the south he gave Shakespeare's company a patent which established its royal title. The document was issued to Lawrence Fletcher, William Shakespeare, Richard Burbage, Augustine Phillips, John Heminge, Henry Condell, William Sly, Robert Armin, Richard Cowley, and the rest of their associates. They were made Grooms of the Bedchamber and were under orders to play when and where commanded. In finance they were generously treated and, with their assured status, they were in a stronger position than they had been under the old Queen. During the reign of King James the Court performances were trebled in number, and other London companies were taken under royal protection and made the servants of the Queen and her son, Prince Henry.

In the following year the King's Men were granted scarlet cloth in which to march in a royal procession through London. The presence of Fletcher at the top of the list of players can be explained by the fact that he had been 'comedian to the King' in Scotland. Here was an early example of the favour shown by James to the Scots, who followed him to their advantage and found offices at Court. How the English players received the stranger we do not know. There is no mention of him in the actors' lists or in the roll of principal players given in the First Folio; so he may have been elbowed aside. He may also have been past his best, with his health already failing: four years later he was buried in Southwark with 'an afternoon knell of the great bell'.

James brought with him to the English throne a gay and extravagant wife, Anne of Denmark, who loved masques and took a happy part in them. Many plays were given at the Court of King James in the winter of 1604, and it is interesting to notice the selected pieces. They were *Othello*, *The Merry Wives of Windsor*, *Measure for Measure*, *The Comedy of Errors*, *Love's Labour's Lost*, *Henry V*, and *The Merchant of Venice*. The last of these was commanded to be repeated on successive nights. *King Lear* was presented at the Christmas of 1606. Since we are so much accustomed to the staging of pantomimes and very light entertainments at that time, the presentation of the most terrifying of Shakespeare's tragedies at such a season shows that James did not at all resemble

Polonius with his taste for jigs and such : evidently he could garnish a feast with a tragedy and did not insist on ' A Christmas comedy ' as companion to the revels of the season.

But there was an ugly side to the new gaiety. Elizabeth had been thrifty to the verge of tight-fistedness : James, in the pursuit of his pleasures, was prodigal. This was agreeable to the players, but not to the taxpayers who heard of huge sums being lavished on the Court masques and heard also of violent debauches during the nights of royal revel. The Court, indeed, became morally degraded ; statesmen were replaced by intriguers, and power passed from the Privy Council to a private clique. The dominion of the Cecils may have been narrow but it had been used for the strengthening of the nation. It ended with the death of the prudent Sir Robert, and a jumped-up Scottish page, Robert Carr, was installed in authority. Carr, who was made Earl of Rochester, was subsequently involved in conspiracy and murder. He was followed in the King's favour by a handsome upstart called George Villiers who rose to be Duke of Buckingham. Those who wished to gain any political or private purpose, had to go on their knees and with a bribe in their hand to this Duke, of whom the historian Clarendon wrote that never had any man in any age risen to such greatness of fortune and of power with so little, beyond his good looks, to recommend him.

There had been a vogue of melancholy in the last decade of Elizabeth's reign. There are fashions in feeling as in clothing. The melancholy Jacques in *As You Like It* is an example of that ' humour ' ; he is grateful for anything that prompts him to more gloom. He can ' suck melancholy from a song, as a weasel sucks eggs ' and he can indeed suck sadness from all the spectacle of life.

> Thus most invectively he pierceth through
> The body of the country, city, court,
> Yea, and of his own life.

But what was an affectation and a species of self-indulgence in self-pity in the case of Jacques and his kind was turned to a far more genuine and far-reaching despair in the reign of King James. Now it was felt that the world, instead of expanding in glory, was contracting in disillusion.

Confidence had been the staple of the Elizabethan character ; but confidence was broken by the impact of corruption on public life. Brooding upon sins became more common than stirring to action. Dr Johnson wrote of the years that were just beginning, 'There prevailed an opinion that the world was in its decay and that we have had the misfortune to be produced in the decrepitude of Nature. It was suspected that the whole creation languished, that neither trees nor animals had the height of their precedessors and that everything was sinking by daily diminution.' Sir Walter Raleigh in his *History of the World* expressed his opinion that 'the long day of mankind draws fast towards its evening and the world's tragedy and time are near at an end'. Chief among the melancholy prophets was John Donne, Dean of St Paul's, remarkable both as poet and preacher. He saw 'the seasons of the year irregular and distempered : the sun fainter and languishing : men less in stature and shorter lived. No addition, but only every year new sorts of worms and flies and sickness, which argue more and more putrefaction of which they are engendered.'

This misery was, no doubt, that of an intellectual minority. The people of the countryside still had their sports and were encouraged by royal command to practise them on a Sunday. But London, grievously smitten by the plague immediately after the new king's arrival, seemed to have lost nerve and was by no means prompted to recover it by the way in which the Kingdom was being governed. James was a man of learning and rightly praised for a bookish wisdom, but to be called 'the wisest fool in Christendom' involves the charge of an incapacity for adding wise action to wise thought. It certainly was not clemency and it surely was not wisdom to imprison Raleigh, unquestionably one of the ablest of his subjects, for thirteen years in the Tower and finally to permit his execution.

To understand Shakespeare's England in two reigns it is worth while following the fortunes of this philosophic adventurer, who had a wider range of talent, knowledge, and bravery than any other of his time. Raleigh was never widely popular because he was one of the monopolists and made money relentlessly ; also, he stood aloof. John Aubrey described him as 'damnable proud'. He lacked the ability 'to walk with kings and keep the common touch'. 'Rude Rawley' they called him. But he was not only a haughty and amorous fop in the manner of most Elizabethan courtiers : he was expert as poet, chemist, geographer, and historian ; he was skilled in shipbuilding, was a dauntless explorer, and well-proven in command of fighting men on land and sea. Born a Devonian, he kept his West Country speech all his life (1562–1618). He came of the squire class, not of the nobility. He went to Oriel College, Oxford, at sixteen, stayed but a year, and at seventeen was fighting for the Huguenots in the French wars. He had to fight also at home. There was no title, no great wealth behind him, as there was behind Essex, Southampton, and the Cecils. He had to drive his way up through the ranks of pomp and privilege.

After some years in France, reading and thinking as well as learning the craft of war, he had a turn as law-student at the Middle Temple. But he did not study long or seriously. As a man of Devon and a seaman by instinct, he had his eyes upon the Golden West. Oddly, this great voyager was constantly seasick and would not even cross the Thames by wherry and would make for London Bridge.

His loves were England, exploration, colonies, and treasure. His hate was directed against Spain. That hate lasted through his life—and cost him his life too. For James I wanted to reverse the Elizabethan policy and humbly to seek peace with Spain. Raleigh stood rigidly in the way of this policy and paid the supreme penalty.

Seafaring and colonising were then a form of private enterprise, with piracy included. It was the custom to raise capital on a joint-stock basis, build or purchase ships, hire crews, and sail for the Americas. Such a trading party might land and pillage Spanish settlements ; better still, it might capture the Spanish galleons returning eastwards, laden with the wealth of the Indies. Later, at home, there was a share-out of the plunder. Queen Elizabeth herself often invested in the adventures and she expected a high dividend. Raleigh and his half-brother, Sir Humphrey Gilbert, were engaged on one of these schemes in 1579. The Spaniards and the weather were too much for them. This early failure did not break Raleigh's belief in an English future on the Spanish Main. But for a while he found work in Ireland, where he crushed a revolt with great severity.

During the following years Raleigh was in favour with the Queen, but not with her statesmen. He was granted huge estates in Ireland ; he had his monopolies, exclusive rights in the sale of wine, broad-cloth, and tin. He had a mansion, Durham House, in the Strand. Most dear to him was the Manor of Sherborne in Dorset, which he made his country home. He was appointed Captain of the Yeomen of the Guard. He was fantastically lavish and was famed for his bejewelled clothes : even his shoes sparkled with gems. But the Queen, alive to his uncommon qualities, was aware that he lacked common sense. She allowed him no position of real authority : even at sea he was foolishly distrusted. He was given no command in the fleet that broke the Armada. So, when another and younger and no less fascinating figure arrived in the person of the Earl of Essex, Raleigh was out of favour. In 1589

one courtier wrote, 'My Lord of Essex hath chased Raleigh from the Court'.

In his leisure he wrote poetry of the highest quality and practised philosophy. His speculations were suspect. Might he not be an atheist and a spreader of damnable doctrine? An inquiry was set on foot by his enemies. It came to nothing; but mud, once thrown, sticks. The attack seems

Above: Sir Walter Raleigh
'In life's uncertain voyage'
       Timon of Athens

Right: The Earl of Essex
'His rash fierce blaze of riot'
       Richard II

ridiculous now : the kind of Christianity to be observed in public life at that time contained little of Christ's teaching. It was a warfare of the sects with remorseless persecution as its weapon. If Raleigh saw no merit in that, he was the more civilised and the better Christian.

Soon he tried to realise the great dream of his life, the discovery and capture of El Dorado, the fabulous Golden City in the West. He located it in Guiana and thither, in 1595, he sailed. The expedition involved terrible hardships : it provided no results—at least in bullion. But during his lifetime Raleigh did popularise two imports from America, potatoes and tobacco. He may not have been the first to introduce either, but he made them familiar. With the former he did great service to the common diet, especially in Ireland ; with the latter he delighted the gentry and founded one of the greatest assets of the British Treasury today. Aubrey, writing less than a hundred years later, said that tobacco duty was worth £400,000 a year to the Government, an immense sum then.

In the great and successful raid on Cadiz in 1596 he played a Rear-Admiral's (and an admirable) part. He was wounded in the leg and unrewarded in pocket. His guerdon, as he protested, was only ' poverty and pain ', though in fact he was not poor.

In 1601 Essex at last threw away his premier position in the Queen's favour (and his life as well) by his crazy attempt to lead a popular rising against her. Raleigh, as the rival of Essex, was on the Queen's side, but the all-powerful Cecils were not letting Raleigh exploit this advantage. When James succeeded to the throne in 1603, Raleigh was doomed.

His enemies saw their chance. They poisoned the King's mind against him. He was accused of joining a plot against the King, and also, which was utterly ridiculous, of being on the Spanish and the Catholic side. The trial, in which the Attorney-General, Coke, raged against Raleigh, was a farce. Raleigh, found guilty of high treason, was sentenced to the hideous penalty of being hanged, drawn, and quartered. But the King knew that the persecution of Raleigh was making him unpopular. So there was a reprieve, and there followed thirteen years in the Tower.

The treatment, it is true, was not severe. The prisoner was allowed good rooms, a patch of private garden, and the visits of his wife, who took a house near by. Fortunately he had his own brain for his constant company. This he could employ in a little chemical 'lab'. And then he also set out to do what H. G. Wells did after the First World War. He began to write a History of the World. Marlowe, once Raleigh's friend, wrote the line, 'Infinite riches in a little room'. How true it was to be of Raleigh's brain in his workshop in the Tower! He never finished the History. But in it he included some memorable prose, and especially the magnificent passage on 'eloquent, just, and mighty Death', which 'hast drawn together all the far-stretched greatness, all the pride, cruelty and ambition of man, and covered it all over with these two narrow words, *Hic Jacet.*'

Released at last in 1616, he determined to make his second voyage to El Dorado. He had royal permission, but no encouragement. He failed to capture or colonise Guiana and returned exhausted, impoverished, and mocked. His enemies were immediately at him again. They barked, they bit, and this time they killed. He had never been formally acquitted of treason. The charge still stood and was now sustained. Raleigh, spared hanging, went with the utmost courage to the block. To the executioner he said, when refusing to be blindfolded, 'Think you I fear the shadow of the axe, when I fear not the axe itself?' and then, 'What dost thou fear? Strike, man, strike.' It is to us astounding evidence of the taste and feeling of the time that his widow had her husband's head embalmed and kept it beside her in a leather bag to be buried with her when she died.

Francis Bacon, Baron Verulam
'I stand here for law'
The Merchant of Venice

Modern psychology would call Raleigh 'a divided man'. His life was full of self-contradictions. In his poetry he condemned material success: in life he pursued it. He said, 'To what end were religion, if there were no reward?' Rewards were ever in his mind. But, while all his fellows were fortune-hunters, no other of the sailors and soldiers had his range of erudition and of speculation or his intensity of application. It was well said of him in his day, 'He can toil terribly'. That James, with all his wisdom, could find no use for such a man and permit the waste of his superb qualities is a condemnation of the King. That the nation should not have risen against the gross injustice of his ruin is partly a condemnation of Raleigh's own arrogant disdain of popularity; still more it is an indictment of the political and moral decay that spread its poison steadily during the last years of Shakespeare's life.

Another life, that of Francis Bacon (1561–1626) is worth recording for the light it throws on the high intelligence and far less exalted morality of the time. He was frustrated during the reign of

Elizabeth, but he enjoyed promotion and power when James succeeded her. It was his misuse of that power which led to his fall and his disgrace.

He came of the ruling class : his father, by title Lord Keeper of the Great Seal, was so influential that he was called, along with the great Lord Burghley, one of the ' twin pillars of the State '. His mother and his aunts were famous for their scholarship and knowledge of languages. Young Francis went to Trinity College, Cambridge, at the age of thirteen and left it at sixteen ; he came down from the university with some contempt for the educational system which he had encountered, but at least that system was partly responsible for the formation of a most remarkable mind, if not of a stable character.

He studied law at Gray's Inn and then was apprenticed to diplomacy ; returning home from France, at his father's death, he found his ambitions for a great public career thwarted by a jealous enmity. He practised law ; he sat in Parliament ; the latter involved no great labour since Parliamentary sessions were then so few. But he vexed the Queen and the Cecils by a line that he had taken. Such opposition was fatal to a career. No office came his way, and he joined the malcontents who attached themselves to Essex. But he did not take part in the Essex Revolt ; instead he took a prominent part in the impeachment of the Earl for high treason. Loyalty to friends was never one of Bacon's strong points. His use of leisure, however, was a very strong argument for his extraordinary intellectual abilities. His first volumes of Esssays appeared in 1597 and at once revealed a master of concise, economical prose as well as of a fine and subtle mind. Bacon could pack more pithy wisdom into a page than most men could set down in twenty.

On the succession of James, Bacon at once attached himself to the new King and at last found himself in favour at Court. Profitable office was soon secured. He was made Solicitor-General in 1607, Attorney-General in 1613, and Keeper of the Great Seal in 1617. The supreme honour came in 1618 when he was made Lord Chancellor with the title of Lord Verulam. (Verulamium was the Roman name for St Albans near which he lived.) But the corruption of the times corrupted Bacon also. He was convicted of taking bribes, fined the enormous sum of £40,000, and sentenced to imprisonment in the Tower during the King's pleasure. As Lord Chancellor he was supposedly the country's chief fountain of justice, and as essayist he had written of that fountain as hallowed and only to be fouled by the vilest of men. He had, before that, lent himself to the prosecution of Raleigh on an absurd charge of treason. Raleigh's crime was to combat Spain when the King wanted peace. Bacon's crime was to procure the judicial murder of a great and innocent man.

He was seemingly ruined, a prisoner for life. But James stood by him, remitted his fine, and ordered his release from the Tower. But while there could be no more public life for Bacon, his private life was magnificently employed with the pen. He retired to his country house near St Albans and added famous books on history and philosophy to a mass of such work already achieved. Nobody could impugn his mental capacities : all could deplore his lack of moral fibre. His life had begun amid the clashing ambitions of the Elizabethans which did at least exhale the clear and bracing air of vigorous rivalry without the grosser forms of dishonesty and speculation ; it closed amid the miasma of moral decadence which James and his favourites had brought to the seats of power.

A typical example of the moral decay of the Court was to be found in the Overbury murder case. There had been an illustrious and extravagantly celebrated wedding in 1605, that of the young Earl of Essex, son of Queen Elizabeth's turbulent rebel, and Lady

Frances Howard, daughter of the Lord Chamberlain, the Earl of
Suffolk. They were both still in their early teens, but youth,
as we have seen, matured much more quickly then than
now. And both were soon ready to be contemptuous of moral
scruples.

Disaster came through the good looks of the King's favourite,
Robert Carr. The young Countess of Essex was fatally fascinated by
him. A lawyer and essayist, Sir Thomas Overbury, friendly to Carr,
warned him that he was playing with fire, but it was Overbury
who was burned. Carr, furious at the description of Lady Frances
as wanton, had Overbury sent to the Tower on the trumped-up
charge of insulting the King, and in the Tower Overbury suddenly
died. That he had been murdered was proved later. Meanwhile
Lady Essex had obtained a divorce and married Carr. There was
no modesty in the celebration of the match, for which sumptuous
masquing was prepared.

Before long, however, the suspicions about Overbury's disappearance rose to a storm and action had to be taken. It was
shown that the dead man had been poisoned with the agreement
of the Governor of the prison and the aid of an apothecary.
Four of those involved in procuring and giving the poison were
hanged. Carr, now Earl of Somerset, claimed to be innocent,
but Lady Frances pleaded guilty. Obviously her husband could
hardly escape condemnation as an accessory : the couple went
to the Tower for six years. It is small wonder that Sir Walter
Raleigh in a bitter poem called *The Lie* wrote

> Go, soul, the body's guest,
>   Upon a thankless arrant ;
> Fear not to touch the best ;
>   The truth shall be thy warrant :
> Go, since I needs must die,
> And give the world the lie.

Say to the Court, it glows
    And shines like rotten wood ;
Say to the Church, it shows
    What's good, and doth no good :
If Church and Court reply,
Then give them both the lie.

Tell men of high condition
    That manage the estate,
Their purpose is ambition,
    Their practice only hate :
And if they once reply,
Then give them all the lie.

The Overbury scandal was the talk of the town during the last years of Shakespeare's life. Some years earlier Shakespeare had written (or contributed to) *Timon of Athens*, a tragedy voicing the blackest despair, contempt for the toadies in high places, loathing of the corrupting power of gold, and general hatred of mankind. Here is a specimen of his declamation :

Who dares, who dares,
In purity of manhood stand upright,
And say, ' This man's a flatterer ? ' If one be,
So are they all ; for every grise [1] of fortune
Is smooth'd by that below : the learned pate
Ducks to the golden fool : all is oblique ;
There's nothing level in our cursed natures
But direct villainy. Therefore, be abhorr'd
All feasts, societies, and throngs of men !

Time and again in the later plays Shakespeare railed at the fawning and cringing before base authority. In his final paroxysm of world-hatred, Timon cries out that robbery is the ruling principle of social life.

[1] Grise means step

I'll example you with thievery :
The sun's a thief, and with his great attraction
Robs the vast sea ; the moon's an arrant thief,
And her pale fire she snatches from the sun ;
The sea's a thief, whose liquid surge resolves
The moon into salt tears ; the earth's a thief,
That feeds and breeds by a composture stolen
From general excrement, each thing's a thief ;
The laws, your curb and whip, in their rough power
Have uncheck'd theft. Love not yourselves ; away !
Rob one another. There's more gold. Cut throats ;
All that you meet are thieves.

Timon, admittedly, is a character in a play, a character who has
been betrayed in his poverty by those who flattered him in his
prosperity. We cannot assume that a character's opinions are also
the dramatist's, but Shakespeare, one may surmise, would hardly
have written with such intensity and ferocity of feeling if he had
not himself been disillusioned to the verge of frantic pessimism by
the changing code of conduct in high places. There is no record
of any performance of *Timon* in Shakespeare's time. It certainly
would have been a dangerous exhibit at the Court of King James.

In February 1613 Princess Elizabeth, the daughter of King James,
was married in state to Frederick V, Elector Palatine. James, whatever his own qualities, could beget children of rare charm. Elizabeth,
crowned Queen of Bohemia in 1619, was a girl brilliant and beloved
and it was not merely the vice of flattery that prompted Sir Henry
Wotton to liken her, in a well-known lyric, to the moon among
stars.

You meaner beauties of the night,
That poorly satisfy our eyes
More by your number than your light,
You common people of the skies ;
What are you when the moon shall rise ? . . . .

So, when my mistress shall be seen
In form and beauty of her mind,
By virtue first, then choice, a Queen,
Tell me if she were not design'd
Th' eclipse and glory of her kind.

This wedding was later on to guarantee the Protestant succession
and bring the House of Hanover to the British throne. Elizabeth's
daughter Sophia married the Elector of Hanover and their son
became our George I. Therefore to that marriage in 1613 we owe
the succession of our own Royal Family, our present Queen being
directly descended from Elizabeth of Bohemia, as she was widely
called.

The betrothal of Elizabeth to Frederick was richly celebrated at
Court, and eight of Shakespeare's plays were performed for the high
occasion, including *The Tempest*, whose masque was probably introduced to strike the matrimonial note.

Honour, riches, marriage-blessing,
Long continuance, and increasing,
Hourly joys be still upon you !
Juno sings her blessings on you.

' Long continuance ' of succession there has been.

But even that happy event had to have its darkening fatality.
The betrothal celebrations were interrupted by the death of Henry,
the Prince of Wales. He was only eighteen when he died as a
result of a fever following a strenuous game of tennis. He had
shown himself able and serious-minded as well as charming. He
was already a keen patron of the arts ; Chapman dedicated his
translation of Homer's *Iliad* to the Prince, and Raleigh, who had
no reason to love the Stuarts, called him ' inestimable ' and ' the
greatest hope of the Christian world '. Had the Prince lived, and
so kept his younger brother Charles from the throne, there might

have been no Civil War and a long and peaceful succession for the Stuarts.

His death interrupted the betrothal revels of his sister. The theatres were temporarily closed. The marriage of Princess Elizabeth did, however, take place in February, 1613, with a profusion of masques, plays, and fireworks. The Thames was illuminated with the discharge of fire-balls from four castles floating on the water ; there was a set-piece of St George and the Dragon and another, since the King loved hunting, of a blazing stag chased into the river.

The times were dark for many, but the torches of festivity were kept flaming. The Court did not only shine like the rotten wood of Raleigh's angry poem. It could light up the town.

CHAPTER TEN

Within a Lifetime

HOW much had England altered within the fifty-two years of Shakespeare's life ? We have noticed decay at the summit of society, but there were many notable achievements during the reign of King James, and their general greatness should not be overshadowed by the spread of darkness in some high places.

The English language went from strength to strength as a means of expression. We think of Shakespeare as an Elizabethan, but much of his most powerful writing was, in fact, Jacobean. The poets abounded, but it was in prose that the early years of the seventeenth century were especially fruitful. Shakespeare in youth had seen and partly followed the fashion for an artificial and patterned style ; it was called Euphuism after the book *Euphues* written by John Lyly (1554–1606). In his comedy of *Love's Labour's Lost* Shakespeare had exemplified the pedantic and over-laden speech self-consciously employed by those who were as ready to play the dandy with words as were the courtiers with their costumes. Holofernes, the school-master in the play, took an absurd delight in verbal elaboration and repetition. He would speak nothing ordinary. The afternoon had to be called ' the posteriors of thē day '. Each phrase had to be balanced. ' Your reasons at dinner have been sharp and sententious, pleasant without scurrility, witty without affectation, audacious without impudency, learned without opinion, and strange without heresy.' In this mode of speech people could not be plainly called this or that. They were ' intituled and nominated '.

Against this buzz of pretentious scholarship the central character of the play, Berowne, at last rebels and one feels that Shakespeare is here speaking for himself :

Taffeta phrases, silken terms precise,
Three-pil'd hyperboles, spruce affectation,
Figures pedantical ; these summer flies
Have blown me full of maggot ostentation :
I do forswear them ; . . .

Henceforth there would be honest, plain speech. In this honesty
the English prose later written was to be singularly rich. It forswore
its foppery.

Jacobean English is seen in its most superb form in the Authorised
Version of the Bible, which drew upon and fortified the English of
previous versions. King James commanded the scholars of the
universities and of the capital to make one abiding Book out of
the existing texts, improving the translation in accuracy. The
betterment, when it came in 1611, was wider than that. The new
Bible was the product of nearly fifty men of learning, seeking
' the truth rather than their own praise ' and all ready to work
with the utmost diligence to achieve a unified correctness. They
would revise their own labours as well as those of others. They
would gladly ' bring back to the anvil that which they had
hammered '. The result of this toil at the scriptural forge we know.

It came too late to influence Shakespeare's own style ; but he
had received plentiful benefit from the Bibles available in his boyhood and youth. The Great Bible of 1539 had been largely sup-
planted by the Genevan Bible of 1560. (This has also been known
as the Breeches Bible because Adam and Eve were described in
it as making for themselves breeches of fig leaves.) This version
was very popular with the Puritans, but was not accepted in the
established churches. Yet, being presented, with pictures, in a
more easily readable form than its predecessor, it had general
acceptance. There are many signs in Shakespeare's work that he
was well acquainted with it.

Linked with Cranmer's *Book of Common Prayer* it had a powerful influence by accustoming the ears of the people to a grandeur of speech which had a strong simplicity as well as a wide vocabulary. Archbishop Parker ordered the so-called Bishops' Bible, which appeared in 1568 and was more to the taste of the orthodox churchmen. But the Genevan Bible was not ousted until the Authorised Version arrived. The name of King James appears, with much flattery which now seems gross, in the dedication, but he had earned some of it. 'Your Majesty did never desist to urge and excite those to whom it was commanded that the work might be hastened and the business expedited in so decent a manner as a matter of such importance might justly require.' The translators were properly grateful for 'Your Majesty's grace and favour which will ever give countenance to honest and Christian endeavours against bitter censures and uncharitable imputations.'

The dedication expressed the fear that 'upon the setting of that bright Occidental Star, Queen Elizabeth of most happy memory, some thick and palpable clouds of darkness would so have overshadowed this land that men should have been in doubt which way they should walk.' There is allusion also to a dread of 'Popish Persons'. But the religious strife to come was far more between the Protestant sects than between Britain and Rome. The folly and failure of the Gunpowder Plot in 1605 to blast the Houses of Parliament, had blasted the future of any Catholic rebellion against King James.

Shakespeare's own town was, by chance, concerned in the beginnings of the Plot. He himself had taken over New Place, which had been the home of the Clopton family in the centre of Stratford: Clopton House, just outside it, had a new tenant in Ambrose Rookwood, who was an ardent Catholic and ready for violent action. The conspirators, including Robert Catesby and others, met at Clopton House and planned for armed insur-

One of the earliest rockets depicted by Hanzelet
‘ A space for further travel’—*Antony and Cleopatra*

rection in Warwickshire after the main blow had been struck at Westminster. Their most important ally was a Yorkshireman called Guy Fawkes who has remained in the sinister limelight ever since. He has won a curious immortality as ‘ the Guy ’ whose image, in various forms, is annually carted round the streets on 5 November and made an excuse for juvenile begging. Fawkes, who had learned how to lay explosive mines in the army, had bored his way into a cellar and hidden two tons of gunpowder under the House of Lords where the opening of Parliament was to be made by the King. ‘ The mines is not according to the discipline of the war,’ Fluellen had said in *Henry V* some years before Fawkes laid his also unmilitary charges.

Fortunately an informer gave away the murderous scheme. The

Lord Chamberlain made a search of the cellars in time and discovered the powder. Fawkes was arrested. The rebellion in the Midlands fizzled out with some minor fighting in which Catesby was killed. Fawkes and Rookwood were later executed with the usual attendant horrors of drawing and quartering. Father Henry Garnet, head of the Jesuit mission in England, was also privy to the plot. He hid for some time, but he surrendered later and defended himself at his trial with arguments which were called 'equivocal'. His courage was not in question. The Porter says in *Macbeth*, ' Faith, here's an equivocator that could swear in both the scales against either scale, who committed treason enough for God's sake, yet could not equivocate to heaven '. This is generally taken as a comment on the trial and hanging of Garnet for treason in May of the next year. If Shakespeare had been, as some argue, an ardent Catholic, he would hardly have put this taunt into a play of his. It can be replied that, since there were some later and generally admitted additions by another hand to the text of *Macbeth*, this may be somebody else's notion of a jest, perhaps one of the remarks inserted by a gagging actor of comedy parts to Shakespeare's disgust.

The occurrence of a Catholic revolt and the threat to his own life, for whose safety he took constant precautions, did not deflect the King from his eagerness to keep the peace with Spain. It was not a complete peace, for the sailors who sought wealth in the West Indies were armed for conflict and ready to do battle for their booty. But the existence of a partial peace gave restless and ambitious spirits more opportunity to pursue their adventures in settlement and colonisation. It was realised that brawling with the Spaniards in the Spanish Main was not the only approach to a brave (and rewarding) new world. There were ample territories to the north.

When Shakespeare was only nineteen, a daring journey was

Fishing in Virginia, 1585

made across the Atlantic. In 1583 Sir Humphrey Gilbert had landed on and annexed Newfoundland, but the difficulties were severe and the settlement abandoned. Two years later Raleigh had made an equally abortive effort to colonise a strip of the east coast of North America which he called Virginia. One of the party, John White, made and brought home a map of the territory.

It was in the reign of King James that success began to be achieved. A niche in Virginia was effectively held in 1606. Two of Shakespeare's patrons, the Earls of Southampton and Pembroke, were members of the Council of the Virginia Company which developed this acquisition. Southampton was a keen backer of trans-Atlantic travel and trade, and Pembroke made a considerable investment in these speculative voyages. The King himself had no colonial policy since he feared Spanish resentment and counter-measures. The intending colonists and their supporters were engaged in private enterprise.

Southampton had given aid to a Captain Gosnold who explored the shores of what was later to be New England. By 1609 Virginia was sufficiently settled to need a governing council, and soon there was a Patriot Party which stood for colonial rights and charters for guarantee of local liberties. Shakespeare must have known a good deal about this and he would surely have approved it, since he was early an advocate of foreign travel and fortune-seeking in the larger world. Sir Henry Rainford, squire of the beautiful village of Clifford Chambers, two miles south of Stratford, and a patron of poets, was a member of the Virginia Company. So was Sir Dudley Digges, elder brother of Leonard Digges who wrote a tribute in verse for the First Folio edition of Shakespeare's plays. Moreover, it was from inside knowledge of one voyage that Shakespeare drew much material for *The Tempest*.

In June 1609 ' seven good ships and two pinnaces ' left Plymouth for Virginia. On the flagship, the *Sea Venture*, sailed Sir George Somers, Admiral of the Virginia Company, and Sir Thomas Gates, who was going out to govern the Colony. They were taking much needed supplies to the settlers. A hurricane overtook them, and the *Sea Venture* arrived, battered and almost sinking, at the Bermudas. The ship went on the rocks, but the crew and passengers were able to land. They had feared ' dangerous and dreaded islands ' haunted by devils, but they found fresh water and abundance of food, including wild pigs and all kinds of fruit and fish. Here, in short, were admirable winter quarters. Out of the timbers of their wrecked vessel the crew were able to build two new pinnaces. In these they successfully sailed, when summer came, to their goal in Virginia, where the other vessels had previously arrived after weathering the storm. The settlers were found to be suffering great privation and were given what help was possible.

Somers returned to the Bermudas, where he may have arrived with too good an appetite, since he is said to have died of a surfeit of the native pork. Gates came back to England to inform the Virginia Council about the state of affairs. He brought with him an account of his party's adventures written by one William Strachey and called *A True Reportory of the Wrack*. This was not published openly for some years, but circulated to members of the Council. One of its members must have given Shakespeare a chance to read it and to take dramatic advantage of its remarkable contents. The description of the storm and of the conditions on the island, where Gates and his men had wintered, has so much in common with the details given in *The Tempest* that Shakespeare's use of Strachey's manuscript seems certain. The island of the play should have been in the Mediterranean since it was encountered during a voyage from Naples to Tunis in Africa. But Shakespeare had hit upon such attractive material in the Bermuda story that he appears to have transferred his scene across the Atlantic.

Another such enterprise probably known to Shakespeare is to be found in William Parry's account, published in 1601, of *The Travels of Sir Anthony Shirley, Knight* who had made most daring journeys in Persia and Russia. During Shakespeare's lifetime the audacity and range of voyaging of the seekers after new and strange lands had steadily grown both in the East and in the West. This tenacity of exploration was to be continued throughout the reigns of the Stuarts. What seems to be an allusion to this expansion is contained in Archbishop Cranmer's speech in *Henry VIII* (Act V, Scene IV). The Princess Elizabeth is being christened and a glorious future foretold for the country when she is queen. Not only will ' good grow with her ', but she will bequeath peace and posterity to her successor. Further, there is a prophecy concerning James which applies to the colonist settlers :

> Wherever the bright sun of heaven shall shine,
> His honour and the greatness of his name
> Shall be, and make new nations ; he shall flourish,
> And, like a mountain cedar, reach his branches
> To all the plains about him.

'New Nations' were scarcely envisaged by that King, but, if we consider the years in the light of the centuries, that forecast was remarkably accurate.

At home there was arriving a new kind of prosperity : the explorers and the colonisers were typical of the Elizabethan spirit in their gallantry, of the Jacobean in their show of commercial initiative. The mediaeval way of life had passed : that economy had been based on the feudalism of the countryside and on the craft guilds, with their regulation of standards and of prices, in the towns. The merchant adventurer, breaking away from custom and control, was now driving ahead as an enterprising individualist. On the land, the new sheep-farming fed the new wealth of the weavers ; at sea the ships sailed out to new horizons ; in the city the capitalist system, with freedom of trade its method and the making of profits its stimulus, was broadening the road to personal fortunes as well as to a greater production of goods.

The writers of plays, ballads, and satires were not economists and their eyes were on the immediate social scene and not on the possibility of any gain to the community. If what we call 'consumer goods' were to become more varied and more plentiful, that was a future benefit beyond their vision. What they saw and what they furiously scolded was the growth of greed, the pomps and vanities of the new rich, and the passing of an old order in which 'degree' had been sovereign and financial acumen had counted for much less than social rank. Ben Jonson was a dramatist who belonged essentially to his own time and was constantly concerned with the horrors, as well as the humours, of the prevailing avarice. Satire demands sin for its subject and comedy is much easier to create by laughing at a vice than by appreciating a virtue. Hence the choice of villainy for a theme. But the villains of the Jacobean stage were not those of Shakespearian drama in which excess of the universal failings of mankind, jealousy, vanity, lust, and excessive ambition had been revealed as the causes of human disaster ; the new targets were the particular offenders of the here and now, the acquisitive Jacobean upstart and the relentless devotee of getting on and getting rich. The ' projectors ', as the men of commercial enterprise were called, were denied any merit of energy and brains ; they were seen only as the servants of Mammon, pitiless in their methods, crude in their appetites, and repulsive in their self-indulgence.

A famous ballad called *The Old Courtier of the Queen's* contrasted that gentleman

> Who kept an old house, at a bountiful rate,
> With an old porter to relieve poor people at his gate

with *The New Courtier of the King's*

> A new flourishing gallant, new come to his land,
> Who kept a brace of painted creatures to be at his hand,
> And could take up a thousand readily on his new bond,
> And be drunk in a new tavern till he be not able to stand.

It does not strike us as good verse : but the picture is vivid. The New Courtier has purchased titles (King James was ready to sell them) and has everything new about him, clothes, servants, pictures, furnishings. He does not, like the Old Courtier, keep to the country in the winter and entertain the neighbours with music, cakes and ale. Instead,

> With a new fashion when Christmas is coming on,
> With a new journey to London they must all be gone,
> Leaving none to keep in the country but his new man John,
> Who relieves the poor people with the thump of a stone.

The New Rich are always an easy object of ridicule by those who have been brought up with other values and have failed, or refused, to see that times are changing and to adapt themselves to the fresh conditions. If we are to judge Jacobean life fairly we must not be too much impressed by the anger of the ballad-makers, which contained a good deal of snobbery, and by the huge output of plays in which the ' projector ' was presented as a mere swindler, as in Ben Johnson's *The Alchemist*, or as a merciless scoundrel like Sir Giles Overreach. This financial ogre was the central figure of a famous comedy by Philip Massinger (1583–1640) called *A New Way to Pay Old Debts*.

The dramatists had their eye on that half of the picture which provided them with a spectacle of human sharks ravening at large among the small fish of the community. The shark and his victims made ' good theatre '. There was, however, the other half of the social landscape. In the welter of new enterprises useful things were being done. Jonson's Sir Epicure Mammon, thinking only of his luxuries, was an outsize cartoon of the gilded knight, hideously fatted with the new wealth. There was also the man of business and affairs whose activities brought genuine social gains and could fairly be called progressive.

Such a one was Sir Hugh Myddelton (1560–1631), the first man to give London a proper water-supply ; it was not a utility which Shakespeare could enjoy since he retired to Stratford before Myddelton's New River was yielding its untainted streams ; but it was a blessing to Jacobean London and has continued to be of value ever since. In Shakespeare's time London drew water from the Thames which was not as much fouled as it is now but offered, nevertheless, a very questionable liquid for drinking. There were also many private wells, and the big houses would thus have their own supply in this way ; but the general public relied on the ' conduits ' which conveyed river or well water in pipes to places whence it could be fetched either by householders themselves or by the professional water-carriers. The word conduit

Paremptitius

Lupos pisces apud Anglos.

A water–carrier

was several times used by Shakespeare when he was describing
tears or a flow of blood. Juliet is scolded by her father in these
terms.

> How now ! A conduit, girl ? What, still in tears,
> Evermore showering ?

In *Coriolanus* there is mention of the conduits that brought water
to Rome. Shakespeare's London was probably less well supplied
with water than ancient Rome herself. The water-porters used
large wooden and iron-bound vessels called tankards, holding
about three gallons ; the men were known as Cobs and there
is a character of this calling named Cob in Ben Jonson's *Every*

Man in his Humour; he lived 'at the sign of the Water Tankard, hard by the Green Lattice'. The carrying of water was a thirsty business in hot weather and so water led to ale, and produced its own taverns. Platter, in his travel-notes on London life, wrote of well-sealed stone cisterns which held the water brought up by the conduits. It was then let off through taps into the tankards carried by the Cobs and so laboriously distributed.

Well sealed or not, the contents of the cisterns can hardly have been a satisfactory source of refreshment, and Sir Hugh Myddelton's determination at last provided a much better one. He was the son of a member of Parliament who had been Governor of Denbigh Castle in Wales. Coming to London for a career, Hugh went into a goldsmith's business and then into banking. He also developed copper-mining in the Welsh mountains. He was a friend of Sir Walter Raleigh and is said to have shared a taste for tobacco; he also shared that inventive man's taste for new ideas and new practices. Hence came the New River, which can still be seen flowing through Highbury and Canonbury in North London and brings water from the north to add to the now far greater resources of the Metropolitan Water Board.

In 1609 Myddelton contracted with the Corporation of the City to undertake the much-needed task of bringing pure water to London. This required a big investment of capital, for the channel to be dug was thirty-eight miles long, bringing down the flow of the Hertfordshire springs into Clerkenwell. There were no mechanical aids to digging then and large numbers of labourers were engaged on the spade-work for four of five years.

Myddelton had to fight reluctant country landlords who resisted the trenching of their fields and the foolish timidity of the City Corporation which would not give aid when the privately invested funds were exhausted. He then turned to the King, who had the good sense to see that here was something of immense value to the town and probably profitable too. James became a financial backer and saved the scheme. Later he also fell into the New River when riding to the great house of Theobalds, a property which he favoured for his hunting. The water was half frozen at the time and James must have cursed Myddelton for a while ; but the hope of profits was a consolation.

The New River Reservoir at Clerkenwell was formally opened with a fine flow of clean spring water from the country in September 1613. The hard labour of digging was complete ; but the profits were a long time in coming. Myddelton lived on to see the fruits of his grand project and he is remembered, most properly, by the naming after him of a spacious square on the slopes of Islington and by a statue in Islington Green. The King awarded many knighthoods unworthily, but Myddelton had certainly earned his. We can now see in him a fine example of the ' projectors ' ridiculed in the plays, sometimes no doubt justly but certainly not in the case of the man from Wales who conferred an invaluable service on the city where he led the new kind of industrial and economic undertakings. When we meet the caricatures of the wealthy upstart on the stage we must visualise such men as Myddelton as well as such targets of the satirist as Overreach and Sir Epicure Mammon. In any case, Myddelton had to wait a long time to see a financial return. This was no case of ' getting rich quick '. The boon to the citizens was for years no benefit to its pioneer.

The ballad of *The New Courtier of the King's* sneered at the new hall, new chimneys, new furnishings, and new pictures on which the new rich were spending their money. But here again there was some injustice. The new wealth was being spent when the level of taste remained high and the domestic arts were being practised by architects and other artists of exceptional talent and sometimes even genius. It was fortunate that men were making money when English building was more than worthy of the sums poured into the construction of mansions in the town and manor-houses in the country.

An example of that could have been seen by Shakespeare close to his own home at Stratford. Near by him, to the west, lay the pastures of the Cotswold hills and the quarries of the mellow, almost honey-coloured, Cotswold stone. The sheep-farmers fed the increased demand for textiles with much-valued wool, sending it abroad to the weavers in Europe as well as to the water-mills of their own landscape. The Golden Fleece was no myth of ancient Greece only : it had now become a reality in the English shires. Those who drew the profit considered their latter end as well as their immediate elegance and comfort. Would it not be prudent to spend in the service of God by adding to the beauty of the churches as well as to see to their own earthly state and convenience by the creation of country houses worthy of their broad acres, now so rich in flocks ?

The golden age of Cotswold architecture is put in the sixteenth and seventeenth centuries. The craft, as well as the capital, was there. So was the water-power. Any journey made today across the tumble of wolds that rise, with intervening river-valleys, to a thousand feet in height between the Severn, the Avon, and the ' stripling Thames ', will reveal in nearly every stone-built village both cottages and manors of a man-made beauty which can also be called a natural beauty, since the buildings with their home-cut stone seem to have grown easily from their site instead of being forcibly imposed on it.

The herdsmen and the weavers became busier. With increasing pastoral and industrial wealth the builders in the Cotswolds and other prosperous districts became more ambitious and yet avoided ostentation ; the style was enriched, not vulgarised. The greatest of the London architects, Inigo Jones, was introduced to countryside construction. On the slope of the wolds running down to the level land of the Severn valley is the exquisite house of Stanway which has not only one of the finest of English tithe barns beside it but a noble gateway and gate-house attributed to Inigo Jones.

English architecture was developing rapidly towards the end of Shakespeare's life. It was abandoning the Tudor fashion which created the mediaeval splendour of, for example, Hampton Court, the royal mansion beside the Thames. It was accepting the Italian classical style which, to put it very simply, substituted straight lines and pediments for angularity and turreted buildings. Balance was the essence of it, expressing a balanced life in a reasoning world. A church built in this manner reminds one of an argument for faith. A Gothic cathedral does not argue : it demands unqualified wonder and worship as it soars to heaven. The new type of manor house was made for calm living whereas the Tudor mansion had suggested defence in times far from quiet.

At the beginning of the seventeenth century Inigo Jones (1573–1652) had been working and studying in Europe, and especially in Italy ; he had been deeply impressed by the magnificence of drawing and design achieved by the Italian masters of draughtsmanship and architecture and he resolved to carry his lesson home. Among other tasks he was commissioned by King James to build a new Banqueting House in Whitehall which was completed in 1622, a building whose proportions, 110 feet long, 55 broad, and 55 high, made a pattern commended later on by Horace Walpole as 'a model of the most pure and beautiful taste'. It is now the United Services Museum. Shakespeare did not live to see the look of London rapidly changing under the new influence, but the man who led the reformation of style must have been well-known to him since Inigo Jones was so closely associated with the writers in the preparation and decoration of the Jacobean Court Masques.

Painting of portraits had been mainly regarded as a matter for foreigners. Hans Holbein, a German, had been the accomplished

'An absolute gentleman, full of most excellent differences'—*Hamlet*

Court artist to Henry VIII, and his combined command of line with realisation of personality produced portraiture of imperishable quality. With him we can see straight into the life and mark the lineaments of the times. He was followed by Hans Eworth of Antwerp. One Englishman did attain great eminence in this form of art. That was Nicholas Hilliard, who specialised in miniatures. These midget pictures were easy to carry on the person and could be made into a form of jewellery as well as of portraiture. His work was much favoured by the Court and courtiers and it is very likely that when Hamlet referred to people paying 'twenty, forty, fifty, a hundred ducats a piece for a portrait in little' he was referring to the Hilliard vogue.

It is a great pity that Hilliard did not turn his attention to the writers who would have paid him less but would have enhanced his fame the more. We are familiar with the engraved portrait of Shakespeare himself in the First Folio which was executed by Martin Droeshout, who was the son of a Flemish engraver. He was only fifteen when Shakespeare died and he is supposed to have worked on a previous drawing. It is a lifeless piece of work and makes us the sorrier that Hilliard, much favoured by King James, did not include the King's actor and dramatist in his clientèle. There has been much argument over the validity of the various Shakespeare portraits that have turned up from time to time. Droeshout has the authenticity of being accepted by Shakespeare's own colleagues and editors ; but it is hard to believe that so lively a mind and spirit

Elizabethan Lady

would not have emerged in the features, if a more skilful hand had been at work. Ben Jonson in the verses printed below the portrait seems to have felt that.

> This figure, that thou here seest put,
> It was for gentle Shakespeare cut ;
> Wherein the graver had a strife
> With nature, to out-do the life :
> O, could he but have drawn his wit
> As well in brass, as he hath hit
> His face ; the print would then surpass
> All, that was ever writ in brass.
> But, since he cannot, reader, look,
> Not on his picture, but his book.

This implies that while there is accuracy in the features of the man there is failure to capture the wit, i.e., the genius of the writer.

Another Fleming, Van Dyck, was later to bring portrait painting back to the high level on which Holbein had placed it. The English painters did good work in the country in their own humbler way; they managed to establish a capable school of mural decoration and a relic of this work can be seen by visitors to Stratford on the walls of the White Swan Hotel. In sculpture there had been much skill shown in the making of effigies on tombs, as can be seen in English churches, abbeys, and cathedrals far and wide. But foreign practitioners were strong in competition, and Shakespeare was himself to suffer once more, not by the brilliance of foreign artists but by the dullness of one of them. One of the Flemish family of Jannsen, naturalised as Johnson, executed the unworthy bust to be seen in the church at Stratford.

If the English lagged behind Europe and had to borrow from it in the graphic arts, they more than held their own in the sphere of music. In composing for the lute and madrigal there was skill and taste of the highest order, and the greatest of the musicians were contemporaries of Shakespeare. Thomas Morley (1557–1603) may have composed airs for Shakespeare's songs in the plays, notably 'It was a lover and his lass' in *As You Like It*. The longer-lived William Byrd (1543–1623) was organist of the Chapel Royal and would thus have been working with the Chapel's Company of boy players. John Bull, who was a Professor of Music and a famed composer too, fascinates us by his mixture of a very English name with very Italian looks; his portrait is at Dulwich and this combination of English simplicity and Italian ingenuity to be discovered in the airs (musical) and appearance (physical) of Professor Bull is nicely typical of the Renaissance and its reception in this country.

It is noticeable that women took no professional part in these artistic activities, and there was little or no change in their status during Shakespeare's lifetime. Yet students of Shakespeare's plays might reasonably surmise that women had a great deal of freedom in the society of the period. Certainly they matched their wits with men. The plays are evidence that the men took equality for granted in the banter of revel and courtship. Beatrice could out-point Benedick in the bandying of jests and ' conceits ', as clever sayings were called : she could draw on an advanced education for her nimbleness in conversation. Rosalind has no less ' a greyhound speed of wit ' and knows her classical mythology. Portia too can make classical allusions as well as display her agility of mind in lawyer's gown : she complains that she cannot get on terms with one of her suitors, ' Falconbridge, the young baron of England ', because ' he hath neither Latin nor French nor Italian '—the implica-tion is that she could speak in any of these tongues. Italian would be natural to the Lady of Belmont, but she had ancient and modern tongues, as well as legal shrewdness, at her command.

We do not hear much of schools for girls if we examine Elizabethan education ; but the standard of instruction acquired at home under tutorship in the great houses was extremely high. Not only was the Queen herself a most gifted linguist : young women of the wealthy and ruling class shared her accomplish-ment. The feminine side of Francis Bacon's family was especially learned ; his aunt Mildred was described by the Queen's tutor, Ascham, as the best female Greek scholar in England, while his mother was famous for her theological knowledge and her power to correspond in Greek with erudite Bishops. Sir Philip Sidney's sister, who became the Countess of Pembroke and kept a famous salon at Wilton House, translated a French tragedy on the Roman Antony and was renowned for her ability to compete with the poets and intellectuals whom she entertained.

Yet at the same time the legal position of women was that of complete inferiors, however lofty was their rank or wealthy their estate. Before marriage a woman was an infant in the eyes of the law ; after marriage, which was usually arranged over her head for reasons of policy or finance, she was almost a chattel of her husband; her property was his. Only if he died had the widow some freedom to arrange her own affairs and dispose of her own wealth. There was no outlet for her energies and talents in the professions. That humility of status lasted in the main into the reign of Victoria and, as far as some professions are concerned, even later. It now seems absurd that so much ability and learning should have been wasted. A woman like Portia, Beatrice, or Rosalind could have held office in the State or conducted a private enterprise with far more acuteness of perception and ability in practice than some of the Dukes and Counsellors we meet in the plays. Yet they remained at home to read and talk, despite the wonderful example of capacity shown by the one really free woman of her time, the Queen.

Among the middle class, women were treated only as marriageable assets first and useful housewives afterwards. In a book published in 1631 (*Tom of All Trades* by William Powell) the author announced firmly, ' I like not a female poetess at my hand '. It was implied that an aristocratic lady might toy with the arts. ' But this is not the way to breed a private gentleman's daughter. I would have her breeding like to the Dutch woman's clothing, tending to profit only and comeliness.' One daughter, in Powell's view, should be kept at home. ' Place the other two forth betimes and before they can judge a good manly leg ; the one in the house of some good merchant or citizen of civil and religious government ; the other in the house of some lawyer, some judge, or well-reported justice or gentleman in the country . . . in any of these she may learn what belongs to her improvement.' The subjects permitted are sewing, cooking, and ' all requisites of housewifery '. The girls were to be ' restrained of all rank company and unfitting liberty, which are the overthrow of too many of their sex '.

Shakespeare's elder daughter, Susanna, who married Dr John Hall, was described in her epitaph in Stratford church as ' witty above her sexe ' and ' wise to salvation '. The latter phrase suggests that she accepted her husband's Puritan views ; the former, amplified by the remark that ' something of Shakespeare was in that ', indicates capacity to take a good part in brisk masculine conversation. But there would be no thought of her doing any work except in the home before her wedding at the age of twenty-four.

Women could only earn a creditable living outside the household by taking up humble forms of toil and commerce. The taverns in Shakespeare's plays, both in town and country, have feminine labour as well as male tapsters ; the women made taverners of character. Hostess Quickly of the Boar's Head, Falstaff's favourite ' local ' in Eastcheap, claims to ' be in good name and fame with the best '. ' Marian Hacket, the fat ale wife of Wincot', mentioned in *The Taming of the Shrew*, has the smack of an actual Warwickshire inn-keeper. Wincot may be Wilmcote, the village near Stratford where Shakespeare's mother came from. On the farms, too, women could be employed. The countryside in *As You Like It* and *The Winter's Tale* is obviously English, and it contains shepherdesses as well as shepherds and there is no reason to suppose that they were merely decorative. There were milkmaids who really milked, and in *Antony and Cleopatra* there is mention of the maid that ' milks and does the meanest chores '. But the men were not allowing women to attempt professional careers, on the stage or in medicine or a lawyer's office. The Phebes and Mopsas were a fact, Portia, as a practising lawyer, was a fiction; and so they remained for centuries.

The English countryside was undergoing some changes of wealth and power ; but the general way of life did not greatly alter. We are used to a world of incessant invention ; we expect a new con-trivance every few months to add to our material convenience. But in the seventeenth century much remained as in the sixteenth and was, indeed, to remain until the end of the nineteenth.

Plague and fire returned intermittently and wrought their havoc. The lack of a good water-supply assisted both kinds of disaster. In

MACHINAMENTVM VT NON VVLGARE, SICVT OPINAMVR
ITA SINGVLARE IN EIACVLANDA AQVA, ADVERSVS
INCENDIA; MAXIME CVM FLAMMA SVPERANTE, NVLLI
PROPIVS AD ÆDES PATET ADITVS—

Firefighting with hand-driven pump

the spring of 1597, just after Shakespeare had bought his big new
house in Stratford, there was a renewed invasion of plague which
ran through the Almshouses and the Grammar School. There had
been destructive fires in the town in 1593 and 1594. In the latter
year there had been great devastation in which the Shakespeares'
house, now known as the Birthplace, was lucky to escape the
surrounding conflagrations. In July of 1614 ' within the space of
two hours' there was another outburst which burned fifty-four
dwelling houses, together with barns, stables, and many valuable
stores of hay and corn. With dry weather, a strong wind, thatched
roofs upon timbered houses, and absence of piped water, a little
fire could start a rapidly-spreading and widely-destructive blaze.
If the local ' watch ' could not be organised with more efficient
methods than those of Dogberry, there was little hope of building
up a fire service that could deal quickly and competently with these
misfortunes.

Methods of transport remained unimproved. Shakespeare still

took the jog-trot way on horseback when he visited London, and his son-in-law, Dr Hall, rode to visit his widely-scattered patients. Carriage-travel for long remained too risky. In the eighteenth century it was still true, according to Lord Macaulay, that for travellers London was as far from Reading as his own contemporaries, using the new railways, were from Edinburgh. Now, of course, with flight added to the resources of the railway, Edinburgh is as close to London, for those who can pay the fare, as Stratford was to Coventry for a horseman in the seventeenth century.

Changing methods of agriculture were attempted. One of these involved Shakespeare in his town's long and complicated quarrel about the enclosure of land at Welcombe. One William Combe, member of a prosperous Stratford family, wished to use as pasture some common land. This was against the wishes of the Town Council and of most of the people. There was long wrangling and tempers rose ; it could be urged that enclosure for pasture produced more wealth and food in the end, but enclosure was a word which roused fierce anger among the people, and Combe was frustrated, despite his promises of compensation. Shakespeare, still watching his affairs in London, where he had bought property in Blackfriars, took no very active part in this dispute, though he was concerned as an owner of tithes. In her book *Shakespeare of London*, Marchette Chute, writing as an American, decides that in the defeat of Combe there was ' a final triumph for medievalism ', and adds, ' but even the most determined town council could not banish the principles of modern farming for ever.' Whether or not ' medievalism ' was as bad as she thinks, Stratford, probably typical of general small-town opinion at the time, preferred it to the new ways of ' progressive ' landlordism.

The Puritans had gained ground locally during Shakespeare's lifetime. In his youth troupes of players had been frequent and welcome visitors. But in 1602 it had been decided by the Corporation that ' there shall be no plays or interludes played in the Chamber, the Gild Hall, nor in any part of the House or Court from hence forward ', and it was further resolved that any town official, councillor, or alderman who gave players leave to perform should be fined ten shillings. That was a considerable sum, but it was increased to ten pounds by an edict of 1612. In this severity Stratford was said to be coming into line with ' other well-governed cities and boroughs '.

But within a few years the old desire for entertainment was prevailing over the new discipline. In 1618 players and owners of a puppet show were paid five shillings and three and fourpence for their services. But Shakespeare's own company, the King's Men, when touring in the Midlands in 1622, were paid six shillings for *not* performing in the Guild Hall. This compensation showed kindliness ; but the ban proved the renewed strength of the Puritans in Stratford.

Warwickshire was to be mainly on the side of the Puritans and of Parliament during the Civil War in the reign of Charles I. The first (and indecisive) battle of that dissension took place at Kineton by Edgehill, quite close to Stratford. Yet Charles I's Queen, Henrietta, was quartered for three days during the war in New Place itself, since Mistress Hall was said to favour the Royal side. This was in 1643 ; her husband had died eight years before. The Corporation politely and cautiously no doubt entertained the Queen and her servants to the extent of fifteen pounds.

Shakespeare's own mind was not on local politics and their disputations during the last years of his life. He looked to his own possessions in and around Stratford and he made regular visits to London to keep an eye on his Blackfriars investment and on the players and their fortunes. It was, as we have seen, a masculine world, and it was plain from his will that male succession to his property was his paramount desire. Without a son, he had to

228

leave his belongings to his daughters, chiefly to Mrs Hall, and the bulk of the estate was to go to any son of her own or of her daughter, Elizabeth. If the male succession failed in the Hall family the property would pass to any sons of Shakespeare's second daughter, Judith, who became Mrs Quiney just before his death. Neither Mrs Hall nor her daughter, who married twice, had a son. Judith Quiney had three sons ; but one of them died in infancy and the other two in early manhood. So the hope of Shakespeare's name continuing and of a male descendant owning the houses and lands for which the poet and playwright had thriftily worked was disappointed in the end.

In the earlier discussion of contemporary medicine, mention was made of the death of Shakespeare's son, Hamnet, in 1596, and of the poignant lines about a dying boy in the play of *King John* written about that time. The insistence on male succession in the will must confirm belief that the wound then inflicted on the father was deep and lasting. He had the consolations of material successs ; he prospered and could enjoy such amenities of moderate affluence as life in that time had to offer. It is certain too that he enjoyed the peace and the fertility of his fields and his garden. Flowers were much in his mind during his last years and none has written of the foison, as he called the plenty, of Nature, with more perception and more gratitude. In one of the later plays to which he contributed, *Pericles*, there is a passage certainly coming from his hand, if the feeling and the language be taken as good evidence. The girl Marina says, when attending her mother's tomb,

> No, I will rob Tellus[1] of her weed,
> To strew thy green with flowers, the yellows, blues,
> The purple violets, and marigolds,
> Shall, as a carpet, hang upon thy grave,
> While summer days do last.

[1] Tellus is the earth.

It is worth notice that these lines are echoed in *Cymbeline* when the heroine, who has been pretending to be a boy called Fidele, has been taken for dead and is to be buried.

> With fairest flowers
> While summer lasts, and I live here, Fidele,
> I'll sweeten thy sad grave ; thou shalt not lack
> The flower that's like thy face, pale primrose, nor
> The azur'd hare bell, like thy veins, no, nor
> The leaf of eglantine, whom not to slander,
> Out-sweeten'd not thy breath.

Flowers make the incidental music in the later plays ; it is a melody of happy recurrence.

It may be a sentimental fancy to think of such lines being murmured on the poet's lips and jotted on paper after a summer day's walk to Hamnet's grave in the churchyard beside the Avon. It is a fancy that I choose to hold permissible. At least we know that through all his riper years he was increasingly fascinated by the annual return of Nature's pageantry, as vivid now each May in the fields and flower-beds of Stratford as it was in his lifetime. Much earlier, in the final and exquisite song at the end of *Love's Labour's Lost*, he had sung of Spring in hue :

> When daisies pied and violets blue,
> And lady-smocks all silver-white,
> And cuckoo-buds of yellow hue
> Do paint the meadows with delight.

The colour-scheme, ' the yellows, blues ', is the same. Here were abiding pleasures.

His last plays renew the joy in the spectacle. The London world had altered. The city of his young ambition had become the city of his disenchantment. He had seen courtiers like Essex who, whatever his faults, was in the true sense ' a gallant ', replaced by the new

King's ungallant creatures, such as Carr. He could be grateful to King James for befriending his profession, but he knew what was wrong. He had given voice at times to the most profound pessimism. There are some lines in *Timon of Athens*, not often quoted, which express the uttermost despair. Disillusioned by the treachery of his friends, and at the point of death, Timon cries,

> My long sickness
> Of health and living now begins to mend
> And nothing brings me all things.

This means that others may go and live with man's society for their plague. Timon wants only annihilation. To be healthy and crave life in such a world is surely to be diseased.

But there remained this other world of the small country town, where neighbours had their likeable crotchets and entertaining humours, where even their petty quarrels could be laughable and where, above all, there was much that did not alter. And if, by some miracle, Shakespeare could see them now he would find much that he loved persisting, things of which he was to the end the happy student and superb recorder, human nature in all its aspects and Nature in her paint-box mood, spreading, as always, the ' yellows, blues' in their plenty, ' while summer days do last'.

INDEX